ECUMENISM
& YOUTH

DAVID DEVADAS

ECUMENISM & YOUTH

BOOK SERIES

WCC Publications, Geneva

Cover design: Edwin Hassink

ISBN 2-8254-1146-9

© 1995 WCC Publications, World Council of Churches,
150 route de Ferney, 1211 Geneva 2, Switzerland

No. 65 in the Risk Book series

Printed in Switzerland

Table of Contents

Preface

Searching for Balance: Ecumenical Youth Concerns at Century-End

This book emerged from my experience of the ecumenical global gathering of youth and students (EGGYS), an intense fortnight of interaction with more than five hundred young women and men in the hills of south-east Brazil in July 1993. The young people had gathered there in an attempt to discover an agenda and a vision for the ecumenical movement in the twenty-first century. They came from 101 countries and belonged to a host of Christian communions and a few other faiths. They were drawn from the World Council of Churches, the World Student Christian Federation and its member Student Christian Movements, the World Alliance of Young Men's Christian Associations, the World Young Women's Christian Association, Syndesmos, the Lutheran World Federation, the World Alliance of Reformed Churches and other Christian youth bodies.

Many of the young people were still teenagers; others were in their twenties, and a few in their early thirties. They were leading and promising members of ecumenical groups in their countries but most of them had never before attended such an international conference along with other young people from different backgrounds.

They were a remarkably mature group of young people. The venue offered marvellous opportunities for a great holiday — in the swimming pool, the bar, the hills or the town — but most of them worked with dedication through long hours of meetings, discussions and other exchanges day after day, eager to look for and to find solutions to the problems of their societies and the world.

The organizations they represented were often very different in orientation and in the nature of their work. Some of the WCC-related youth groups were actively engaged in grassroots movements. Others came from the

cloistered environs of theological colleges. Some of the
YMCAs represented were involved in working for social
change, but quite a few of the YWCAs had no activist
background at all. Some Student Christian Movements
such as the one in the Philippines had been engaged in
hard political struggles. Many others were largely meeting
places for Christian youth on campuses. At Mendes,
though, their various backgrounds and experiences were
not barriers; rather, they contributed to making the gathering a truly representative cross-section of the ecumenical
youth movements across the globe.

The gathering was not an historical first. There had
been three earlier gatherings of ecumenical youth. The
first was at Amsterdam in the Netherlands in 1936. The
second, in Oslo, Norway, in 1947, was perhaps the most
seminal such event in the history of the ecumenical
movement; it met just a few months before the foundation
of the World Council of Churches. W.A. Visser 't Hooft,
who became the first general secretary of the WCC, was a
guiding spirit at Oslo, and Philip Potter, the third general
secretary of the WCC, was one of the leading lights,
representing the Student Christian Movement of Jamaica.
The third gathering of ecumenical youth was held at
Kottayam in India in 1952.

All these previous gatherings had been limited to
representatives of predominantly Protestant and Orthodox
organizations. At Mendes, for the first time, representatives of Roman Catholic youth organizations formed
about a third of the total number.

But there was, for the most part, very little consciousness of denominational differences. Language, culture
and the process of preparing for regional cultural programmes made it natural for participants from particular
countries or regions to be together more often than with
others, but on the whole the gathering came together
almost magically as one whole group without barriers or

consciousness of differentness. Work at the gathering, thus, was truly that of global young ecumenists.

Through months and years of painstaking planning, the organizers had achieved a difficult feat. They had been able to bring together in a microcosm the rich diversity of today's ecumenical youth movements in such a way that they could transcend their differences to form an effectively workable, interactive group.

The way the gathering was planned and structured helped to achieve this unity. The young people first congregated in Rio de Janeiro at the beginning of July 1993. There they were divided into groups which travelled for five to six days to various parts of the city or to other cities or rural communities across the vast country. These groups were exposed at first hand to the lives and work of activist groups, indigenous communities, Christian missions of various kinds and ordinary Brazilian families, before they headed for the normally sleepy hill town, Mendes, a few hours' drive from Rio.

There they lived and worked together for ten hectic days of worship, theme presentations, group discussions on a variety of issues and nightly celebrations of the cultures of one continent or another. To help participants cope with the strain of the wide variety of activities that were happening around them, they were organized into small groups which met periodically to gather feedback and assist those who needed support. The sponsoring organizations and some of the church traditions met with representatives of their particular organization or denomination a couple of times but this did not lead to separateness in most of the activities of the gathering. If participants did band together to strategize or for consultation, it was as women or as national or regional groups.

Staff of the international offices of the sponsoring organizations had planned the event over some years. They had identified certain key concerns for discussion at the forums through which participants shared their experiences of and responses to these issues. The six forums, to one or another of which each participant was assigned, dealt with the search for unity in a fragmented world; the rights of people and democracy; women; the economy, society and alternative models; the environment and development; and education for life.

The venue of the gathering a few kilometres from Mendes was run by Marist brothers. Situated in the hills, it provided enough space for those who needed to get away for walks, and for the various meetings that seemed to be going on at all hours — and also for those who wanted to play soccer or relax in some other way. Mendes, of course, became the social centre for the young people.

I was asked by the Communication Office of the World Council of Churches to cover the event for its news agency and monthly magazine and, thereafter, to write a book on the issues of youth today. One of the themes suggested was a vision for the ecumenical movement in the twenty-first century. Covering the event as a journalist was easy enough, but writing a book has been a tough challenge. It took me a long time to understand the message of EGGYS. It was a quiet message, for the young people there were not trumpeting causes or issues and certainly not visions for the next century.

I worked on several drafts before I settled on this pattern. This is not a synthesis of what happened or was said at EGGYS. It is not a report on the event or a summary of the documents which inevitably came out of it. It is a subjective presentation of my understanding of what young people involved or interested in the ecumenical movement are saying — or rather, what they are searching and listening for. It could not have been written, though, without the intense experiences of those fascinating weeks among that cross-section of the ecumenical leaders of tomorrow, working, praying, hearing and sharing together their various realities and backgrounds.

I have tried to see the larger picture put together by the reports of the six forums at which participants at the gathering discussed issues, but I have not restricted myself to that. For this book is an attempt to use my experiences at the gathering and elsewhere to formulate a thesis on the basic unity of the problems that face the generation which was born between 1960 and 1975, and who are within the ecumenical movement in its widest form, as they prepare to enter the next century — a millennium is too much for any one generation to prepare for.

What I have is not a vision for the twenty-first century but a presentation of the basic challenge before this ecumenical generation and, indeed, before every young person who is concerned about equality, and liberation from exploitation and the maintenance of what is left of the integrity of the earth. I want to explore how we may deal with the alienation of so many of us, and ensure that everyone has enough to eat and nobody wastes the earth's bounties for no better reason than to have more.

The challenge is a moral one but it must be faced and answered by young people in various situations in different ways. For it means refusing to use what is easily available to one in economically rich societies and working strenuously to ensure for everyone what is difficult to come by in economically poor societies. The life-styles of some must urgently be enhanced if they are to be freed from exploitation, while the life-styles of others must urgently be curbed if the earth and all that is in it are to survive.

The challenge essentially is to achieve the balance that alone can allow the planet and each of us to survive, and not only to survive but to grow in fullness and in joy.

1. Traumatized Generation

The ecumenical movement may have entered the twentieth century with a clarion call for "the evangelization of the world in this generation" but it is ending the century with far more humility. Not only has it failed to win the world for Christ; the century has seen the most horrifying orgies of mass destruction, the breakdown of community and family life, the aimless alienation of persons within their societies, and the spread of a new plague across the globe. Amid these deadening experiences, perhaps in part because of them, the century has witnessed the marginalization of religion in many societies.

It has been a chastening experience for those who have lived the major portion of their lives during this century. As the second millennium draws to a close, the present is bleak, the future uncertain. For young people, with most of their lives still ahead of them, the prospect of the twenty-first century is filled with foreboding. Those among them who are ecumenically inclined and wish to be missionaries or ministers of one sort or another don't quite know what they will have to offer to those among whom they will minister. Certainly, few within the ecumenical movement still dream of evangelizing the world. More are concerned with stemming the tide of disillusionment and cynicism that has taken more and more people away from the church.

The struggle against apartheid and to initiate dialogue with other living faiths offered areas of thrust during the last third of the twentieth century. Apartheid provided a generation which had been born during the colonial age with a sharply focused area of concern and action. Gradually, however, the issues of racism have become more complex as a wide variety of sometimes subtle ethnic divides have emerged as confrontations. Issues such as migration and nationalism have become deeply intertwined with racism.

The majority of young people with ecumenical convictions today take dialogue with other faiths for granted as a natural and integral part of ecumenism, but dialogue is often daunting in a world riven with ethnic strife and fundamentalist revivalism. For, despite their relative openness and humility compared with earlier generations, most young people today have little patience with even those within the churches and the ecumenical movement whose views tend to be intolerant or narrow. On some matters, young people regret the compromises their parents made and are chary of repeating them. For them, their unwillingness to accept narrow, chauvinistic or exclusivist perspectives is not reverse intolerance. The very survival of the earth appears to them to depend on their strength to love.

Service, aid and charity have all become ambiguous and open to question as young people are faced with the negative aspects of development, industry and wealth, with natural disasters caused by unnatural human behaviour, with evidence that the life-styles of aid-givers are among the causes of the very disasters the effects of which they seek to alleviate. As the patterns of international trade, debt, consumption and pollution are exposed, more and more young people are beginning to realize that they are in a position to undertake charitable work precisely because other people halfway across the globe are denied what they take for granted. Worse, they feel the guilt of exposing those whose life-styles have been most simple and natural to such consequences of their and their forefathers' extravagances as toxic waste and related illnesses, the hole in the ozone layer and global warming.

Young people are beginning to discover that the challenges ahead are far greater, more demanding and more urgent than they have ever been. They see that black and white solutions don't work any longer, that there are at least two and often many aspects to every issue. They realize that human-rights concerns are often used selectively by powerful Northern governments and their communication media to put pressure on emergent economies which could threaten their control over global trade and wealth, and that the same forces gloss over serious violations of human rights elsewhere.

As they grapple with issues that seem more and more like Rubik's Cube, many young people realize that the problems the world faces are very often not external to them, that they cannot simply be agents of change, "civilizing" missionaries. For, all around them, the civilizations which their forebears held to be exemplary are being recognized as destructive, exploitative and sinful. They realize increasingly that their life-styles, their prejudices, their societies, their nations, their churches, contribute in some measure to aggravating the earth's problems.

A quiet mission

The ecumenical mission of the twenty-first century will perhaps therefore be a quiet one. It will listen with concern, watch with caution and speak with a voice laden with guilt. It will seek answers rather than point the road. More and more young people are becoming conscious of the need to minister to themselves, to find the strength and the grace to change their life-styles, to limit themselves, to watch and hear and love.

Justice, peace and the integrity of creation remain challenges but many ecumenical young people the world over are beginning to see these not as external challenges for the church to go out and do something about, as in providing aid to those fighting racism, sending messages to world leaders about conflict situations or planting trees, but as challenges to themselves, to their life-styles. Their mood is introspective. Many of them are looking at themselves, searching for ways to live, act, connect, love and be loved that would make for a more wholesome world. The new heaven and the new earth must come from within, not be created in someone else's space, at someone else's expense.

Ecumenically-minded young people today do not easily get agitated or angry, they are willing to hear another's point of view, they don't seek to score debating points, they tend to believe the next person may have a better idea. Humility, it would seem, is back in Christian life and work. These young people are no revolutionaries. They certainly wouldn't cut through jungles to get to "heathen" villages. Normally, most of them would not even take to the streets to demonstrate on issues of public or private concern as their parents of the "sixties generation" in many parts of the world would have done at the drop of a placard. They do not generally align themselves with political movements or parties.

This is not to say that they are apathetic. Ecumenical youth leaders today are at least as concerned about the injustices, the problems around them, as their grandparents were, probably more deeply so. The difference is that they do not think they can cure these ills through activism or aid. There is a perception of limitation, of inadequacy.

If many of them perceive that the problem is not external to themselves, that it is not by changing someone else that they are going to make the world a better place but by changing themselves, it does not follow that they know how or what they must do. Indeed, they generally don't. Yet they are searching with seriousness. Even those of them who can afford the cheap escapist answers of the 1960s and 1970s — mysticism or drugs or cheap travel to distant lands — have little to do with these. Their search is deeper, and much quieter.

Moral confusion

In a world which is suddenly a smaller, more limited place, absolute answers are elusive. Every pro seems to have a corresponding con. Doing just about anything could be harmful in some way or to someone. It is difficult to distinguish good from bad when everything which once seemed good turns out to have an ugly underside. Take industrial growth. Every generation before this one, ever since the industrial revolution first got revved up, grew up to believe in it as a process that had unlimited potential. Whether the economy was organized on capitalist or communist principles, the road to prosperity was through industry. This generation is the first one ever to have heard more of environmental depredation than of industrial growth since they were little.

Through the 1970s and 1980s, when today's youth were children, it was the games of the stock market — take-over bids, junk bonds and forward trading — which dominated over actual industrial expansion. The world of business looked a lot murkier than it did to previous generations, its successes based on gambling, scheming and double-crossing rather than on hard labour.

The factories this generation heard most about were the nuclear plants at Chernobyl and Three Mile Island, or the Union Carbide factory in Bhopal which spewed poison fumes that killed and maimed thousands in December 1984. Industry was definitely a bad word, business an underhand operation, labour taken for granted. Across the globe, labour movements have been in decline since the 1970s and early 1980s as managers and governments manipulated them in the name of competing with the "labour forces" of other countries to manufacture better and cheaper products faster and using fewer hands.

Anyone born in 1970 would have been too late to have been bombarded with images of Apollo 11 and its astronauts landing on the moon beamed by an energetic

US publicity effort across the non-communist world in 1969. The space venture a 1970s baby would have been conscious of would be the shocking failure of the manned space shuttle in 1986. As the Challenger crashed, the frontiers of human experience and potential didn't seem to be expanding any more. If anything, they seemed to be contracting.

Even until the 1970s, the acquisition of wealth, whether by individuals or corporations, was still considered a desirable objective in most parts of the world. In the 1990s, a large question mark hangs over the morality of driving a car or using an air-conditioner or even plastic bags or paper. Consumption now causes guilt among those who can buy. Yet, it is essential to provide goods to the millions who go hungry. Production cannot be abandoned, yet must be checked. Coping with this conundrum isn't easy for a young person. No adolescent trying to come to terms with his or her life and goals can be sure about how much of what is okay.

The same goes for sex. Just when many parts of the world appeared to have come to terms with sexual freedom, AIDS has made it a taboo, or at least a more fearsome exercise than ever before. For those whose parents' generation romped relatively freely in the 1960s and the 1970s, the new fears are frustrating.

The result of these changes, often devastating for an adolescent's fledgling aspirations, and the accompanying communication revolution, which has brought all these frightening new realities into living rooms even in economically poorer countries, is that young people today know and understand a great deal more than any generation at their age did before them. They are probably more mature than any previous generation might have been but their awareness of failures and reversals, of the limits of growth and the limitations of activism, also means that they don't feel inspired to optimism or the zeal to work for change, for a better world, for the kingdom of God.

Universal discouragement

This trend is not limited to the young people within the ecumenical movement. Across the world, there are few activist student or youth movements that are playing a decisive role in their societies or nations in the 1990s. Firebrand or nationally accepted revolutionary leaders are often middle-aged, having taken the lead in the 1960s or 1970s. Those zealots who are in their teens or their twenties are generally drawn into guerrilla insurgencies but these are mainly ethnic-nationalist or religious-revivalist because there are no exciting ideologies around any more to inspire young people to struggle for a better tomorrow within their nations and societies.

Leftist political activity had been the norm for young people through much of the twentieth century, even though most of them used to settle down to humdrum, relatively conservative lives by the time they took up jobs and marriage. Over the past few years, leftist activity has become *passé* in many parts of the world. The heady days of the Sandinista revolution have given way to a right-wing, pro-US government in Nicaragua. Left-wing ideology has been in retreat, giving way to right-wing economic policies even in China and Vietnam.

The Philippines' people's power, the protests at Tiananmen Square, the student agitations in South Korea, all appear to have subsided, some more than others. The change in South Africa was the last recent inspiring and encouraging event for those who seek a better world, but the end of apartheid also means that a major rallying point for protest action by young people across the world has ceased to be an issue.

The disintegration of the Soviet Union has meant a seminal change in the political environment across the globe. With the end of the bi-polar global cold war, the non-aligned movement came apart. Leftist movements, including many Christian groups in the countries of Latin

America, Asia and elsewhere, found their networks of support had disappeared. Worse, many of them found that they had become objects of ridicule as their cherished alternative models appeared to have failed miserably. A global network of activism, which used to effectively channel the energies, concerns and idealism of many young people in different lands, had collapsed.

At one level, this generation faced the reaction to the idealistic excesses of their parents' generation, which took "flower-power" revolutionary ebullience to the streets in the 1960s but soon dissipated their fervour in drugs, music and psychedelia, not only in many of the countries of the North but also in the upper classes of much of the South.

After that ebullience of the 1960s and 1970s, the 1980s, when today's young people were growing up, witnessed the strengthening of conservative, right-wing regimes in many democracies. The social democrat stream of politics had little to show for itself. Gradually, through the 1980s, more and more poor countries were lured into debt traps and the economic severity dictated by the Bretton Woods institutions, and their governments too have become correspondingly right-wing.

The majority of the richer countries gradually went into a recession which seemed to go on and on. It was not a time when social welfare, travel or exchange sponsorships for students or aid projects in which young people could get involved were easily available. There were few avenues through which the adolescent conscience could be eased.

Changed life-styles

Not only do young people see very little that they can do constructively to change things around them, television has ensured in most countries that children and adolescents have no time even if they wanted to get involved. Soap operas and serials are the new addictions of this generation. Young people routinely spend a large number of hours every day watching programmes which numb the mind to the larger, systemic problems in their societies.

Almost unnoticed, children's life-styles have changed drastically since the 1970s. They tend to spend less time playing, or even going outdoors. Picnics and expeditions are almost concepts from the past for a great many teenagers today. Even outings to the cinema or to live shows or museums or zoos have become relatively uncommon. This is happening not only in the more industrialized countries but also in the fast-expanding cities of predominantly agrarian nations. TV aerials are ubiquitous in shanty towns and slums in just about every city from Manila to Mexico City. Rock music performances may still remain popular outings but probably far fewer young people can play an instrument today than those in their parents' generation could.

It is in this context that most university campuses across the globe have become far more tranquil and apolitical in the late 1980s and early 1990s than they had been over the previous half-century. Students used to believe in causes, in political paths to a better life for all, as long as the goals of industrial growth, technological advancement and higher levels of consumption were unchallenged and seemed morally correct. Whether they chose to get involved through communism, other political parties, volunteer or church action, young people could have a dream, a purpose, a moral tenor to their lives. Today, not only the various paths but also the goals which were once taken for granted are in question. Suddenly, higher levels of consumption seem immoral, industrial growth means environmental depredation.

On the other hand, as global competition for limited markets increases, as economies go into recession, as new technologies lead to higher levels of mechanization and jobs become both more difficult to come by and more lucrative for those who can be achievers in a cut-throat business environment, students look for security much earlier than their forebears did. Looked at another way, they are escaping into the rut, refusing to take any responsibility for the mess around them. After all, being just another brick in the wall lends security, support and strength. The average middle-class teenager in many countries today has already laid out his or her plans for a lucrative future. Most of them make no time to discuss the problems of the world around them, leave alone activism.

Ecumenical role

As their peers rush headlong into the competitive world of good grades, presentability and lucrative jobs, members of ecumenical youth groups and movements have become some of the very few young people who make time for other activities and concerns. In many cases, groups like quite a number of YWCAs have adapted themselves to their environment and try to arm their members with the extra skills that can help them survive in a tough world. There are other ecumenical groups which make time to think about the world around them with concern. Some, though few, are politically activist, but a large number of Roman Catholic groups, WCC-related youth groups and YMCAs in different countries are actively involved with social, cultural and economic issues in their contexts. In some countries of the North, this takes the form of environmental concern and action against racism. Women's rights and the rights of indigenous people are major concerns for many groups across the globe.

In the 1960s and 1970s, secular groups tended to overshadow church groups in the extent of their concern, involvement and activism on these and other, often more political, issues. Today, while the church groups are perhaps only marginally more active than they were then, they are, in some places or universities, among the few youth and student groups that are active at all. Even though the level of grassroot involvement and activism of church-related youth groups may appear to have decreased since the 1970s and 1980s, their importance has increased in relative terms because so many others have ceased to be active.

Since the search of the 1990s is for moral answers to the uncertainties, the dilemmas, of the often-conflicting current concerns, these groups can play a far more important role than church-related groups were able to in the heady days of the 1960s. In order to do this, however, these groups must search for the limits of acceptable consumption, for life-styles that provide for enough human needs to guarantee that the weak in a society will not be exploited, oppressed and deprived, and yet minimize the damage that all consumption necessarily causes to the environment, to the earth and to all other creatures.

Such concerns of the ecumenical activity of the last quarter of the twentieth century as sustainable development and justice, peace and the integrity of creation must seek to provide the answers which those young people who, having resisted the competitive rush of the times, are searching for today. Their search holds up a flame of hope in a discouraging landscape.

2. Web of Problems

It was in the context of this much-reduced level of youth activism across the world and a towering moral crisis before affluent societies, churches and the ecumenical movement itself that some five hundred young people came together for the ecumenical global gathering of youth and students (EGGYS) in July 1993, looking for a vision to inspire the ecumenical movement in the next century. The concerns of many of them were remarkably alike. The similarity of their attitudes and perspectives was obvious in their responses to presentations from keynote speakers. The vast majority of them, it turned out, were involved in a similar sort of search, a search for future options for life — for the earth as a whole and for their societies and contexts.

Perhaps the single most powerful moment of the EGGYS experience came during the closing worship, when some bread and bananas were passed in small baskets around the school basketball court where everyone was assembled. There wasn't all that much food but, responding to the symbolism of this sharing across denominational barriers, the young people broke off little bits of the bananas and passed them further down the rows until, by the time those that wanted to share had taken a bit each, there was much left over. When the participants saw this, the solemnity of the sharing gave way to a wave of joy as some began to dance, and soon almost everyone had joined hands to form chains of young people that swirled joyfully around the little stadium, moving some chairs and winding between others, laughing and singing with abandon.

Perhaps it was because of their youth, but the joy of sharing and the keenness to affirm their togetherness was obvious at each worship service that provided an opportunity for the sharing of the peace. At least ten minutes would be spent as the hundreds of young people, black and white, women and men, Roman Catholic and Lutheran, Quaker and Orthodox, roamed from one end of the worship area to the other, looking for friends, embracing and kissing, saying "shalom", "peace" and "God bless" with a warmth that would be difficult to find at any other such gathering. There were a few separate eucharistic celebrations but many who were not Roman Catholics flocked to the mass outside a grotto on the school campus as their Roman Catholic friends pleaded with them to come and be with them. "But why can't you take communion with me?", a 24-year old Roman Catholic asked a Protestant, thoroughly baffled by such enforced eucharistic isolation.

Mature search

The search for unity was most intense at EGGYS, though without any great declarations or rhetoric. Considering the youth of the participants, the maturity of their search for unity was remarkable. It included an acknowledgment of the things that divide, of the fragmentation in their societies, countries and home situations. There was very little of callow idealism and a great deal of introspective searching. They were a remarkably good set of listeners, willing to hear, appreciate and sympathize — and generally without shrill, impetuous or do-gooder responses.

The vast majority of participants reacted with tumultuous applause to Korean feminist theologian Chung Hyun Kyung's presentation of Asian responses to the crises of the age. Most of the young participants felt keenly the alienation and hopelessness with which the presentation grappled. Barely half a generation away from them, she was able to speak to them in their idiom of her "relationship" with Reggae musician Bob Marley, of the revolting scenes of sex tourism she had witnessed, of her search for God. She spoke of quietude, of the self-control and patience of Asian spirituality, of the divinity within each person and of communion with nature.

The young people themselves spoke of many and varied experiences of despair and fragmentation: racism and violence in South Africa, torture and disappearances in Chile, ethnic discrimination and linguistic problems in Canada, xenophobia in Europe, destruction and the separation of relatives in Lebanon, ethnic war in Sri Lanka, tension between Catholics and Protestants in Colombia, deterioration of the social fabric in Brazil because of external debt. The list seemed endless.

Theirs was obviously a spiritual quest, for they responded with far greater enthusiasm to Prof. Chung's presentations than to others that dealt with economic systems. Most of them had no reservations about her insistence on rooting her personal spirituality in her Korean context. One or another small band of participants appeared to be sitting with her almost constantly during the days of the gathering, under a tree or on the grass, trying to come to terms with their own spiritual journeys.

Strong reaction

A small group of perhaps half a dozen young people from Middle Eastern Orthodox churches did have strong reservations about contextual interpretations of Christian spirituality. For them, Christian practice had to exclude anything that was not a part of church tradition, approved by the councils of church fathers and specifically sanctioned by the Bible. They refused, for instance, to participate in the sharing of bread and bananas during worship even though the gospel allusion with which it was introduced related to the parable of the loaves and the fish and not to the last supper.

Some members of this group strongly opposed contextual interpretations of the gospel and dialogue with people of other faiths. "We have a 2,000-year history of blood and martyrdom and now you want us to go and say, 'It is all forgotten, we have no differences'?", asked a Syrian priest. For many other young people there, however, dialogue was an inseparable part of ecumenism. The vast majority of the gathering was immensely tolerant of divergent views but, after ten days of interaction with the Orthodox group, it became clear that their commitment to their understanding of a liberal, inclusive ecumenism would brook no compromise on such issues and the small Orthodox group was almost excluded by the time the gathering ended.

One of the points on which the Orthodox group did find allies was in its strong opposition to accepting homosexual behaviour. A number of men and women, mainly from Africa, felt as strongly as they did that homosexual activity was sinful. Some African and some Orthodox men were also uneasy with the determined group of young women who spoke strongly of women's exploitation in homes, work-places and churches. However, there seemed to be a broad acceptance of feminist concerns among the large majority of participants.

Gender equality

Indeed, the best indicator of the fact that the next ecumenical generation accepts sexual equality more naturally than any before it was the composition of the gathering. The organizations represented there had sent more women than men. Though the organizers had asked for gender balance when inviting applications, they had not consciously tried to ensure that women outnumbered men. This must surely have been the first conference of this sort which was not concerned exclusively with women's concerns where women had, through the natural process of selection, come to outnumber men.

The organizers of the forum for the discussion of women had probably worked harder than any other to prepare for the gathering. They had held regional gatherings of women and a pre-conference meeting in India, where some of them exchanged experiences of exploitation, repression and violence in homes, offices and churches during what were apparently some very emotional sessions. The bonding that occurred there helped them to make the fastest progress in their forum at Mendes, particularly in the early days when other forums were still coming to grips with the issues before them.

Unity of problems

However, once the young people had analyzed the issues in the different forums, it turned out that most of them saw links between the various kinds of exploitation which plague the world and different societies and regions. The exploitation of women, for example, was associated with the repression of ethnic groups, with racism and the exploitation of poor nations and of the environment.

The forum at which the search for unity in a fragmented world was discussed identified the oppression of women with that of the "third world" and of nature, and called for a struggle "to balance masculinity and femininity in our societies". The forum members' report to the gathering criticized fundamentalism as "a phenomenon of power" which focuses "on a simplistic formula, stressing only three or four basic tenets and ignoring important issues which may arise". The report said racism was not simply a North-South problem but exists in different forms throughout the world. It described ethnocentrism as "a cultural arrogance which maintains the belief that our culture is superior to others. This belief is sustained through a systematic process whereby our values are inculcated in us in our specific cultures through family, school and social circles." It urged a positive view of cultural diversity.

This report held that "under the guise of information distribution, the mass media alienate and perpetuate the dominant ideology through its tendency towards sensationalism and consumerism". About class divisions it noted that poverty, as a social reality, does not derive from capitalism alone, that for reasons such as education and the level of their organization, the most oppressed are not necessarily the ones who struggle most and that class struggle is strongest when it coincides with ethnic and racial struggles.

Fragmentation, it said, results from greed and selfishness, forces people individually and collectively to mistrust "the other" and attempts to establish a homogeneous yet exclusivist culture. It concluded that fragmentation was alienation from God and others as a result of original sin. Unity, then, was an experience that could only be rooted in respect, involving an acceptance of differences in a spirit of trust, honesty and love, allowing for independence and self-determination. It was enriched, not threatened, by diversity. The report described as false any unity which tries to homogenize or is used to manipulate people into passivity and dependence, any unity which hates diversity and is used to promote the values of the powerful. Unity, it emphasized, "is not an event but a daily journey. Sometimes we find it and sometimes it finds us."

Addressing formal ecumenism, it said: "For Christians, unity is commensurate with our faith journey. In this context, we deeply regret that churches have not always shown a paradigm of unity amidst so much fragmentation and that this lack of unity has become a major obstacle in evangelization, prophetic witness and service to the world."

Holistic education

The forum at which education for life was discussed also emphasized the diversity of people and the need for "a holistic education for the individual, which trains one with a critical conscience". Talking of the need for persons to become agents of change, the report said: "We want an education that articulates the means necessary for individuals to be aware of the realities of different countries, the distinct social movements, and then, based on this information, confront their own ideas and have a more critical and constructive view of society."

The forum noted the manipulation of education to perpetuate inequities in societies. In some countries, there were not enough public schools, in others meagre or no provision for secondary education in them, classrooms were not big enough in some, classes were held under trees in others, and teachers underpaid in many. In some, young people were educated to become only manual labourers and not thinking individuals. In those countries where education was free and available to all, it said, students were put under great pressure from an early age and this produced emptiness and stress, resulting in their alienation.

Individualism and greed

The forum on environment and development grappled with the problem of where to draw the line between the enrichment of individual lives and greed. "What God has given us should be used to serve and enrich our lives but should not be used to fulfil our greed and to dominate others. At what point does the usefulness of the natural world become subject to mere expropriation of resources? We question the definitions of development employed by governments and international organizations and seek a new understanding of who should participate in the benefits of technology and capital."

The forum's report emphasized the problems of nuclear dumping, particularly in the Pacific, water pollution, particularly through contamination by toxic chemicals, deforestation which leads to soil erosion, climate change, desertification and diminished natural beauty, population concerns, particularly the need to empower women with education and resources for sustainable development, and the lack of motivation in established networks, international organizations and even churches to deal with these problems.

The forum identified "over-consumption in richer areas of the world which consume proportionately much more than their fair share of the world's resources" and the contradiction between beliefs and actions as basic problems. Like the forum on the struggle for unity in a fragmented world, this forum too saw relationships between the various apparently unrelated problems of the time. It held that "only by understanding the inter-relations between poverty, environmental degradation, the status of women and the hegemony of capitalism are we empowered to act and to convince others to be protagonists in effecting change".

Building the kingdom

The report of the forum on economy, society and alternative models affirmed their Christian belief that people are created to work with God to build the kingdom rather than to acquire power and accumulate riches for themselves. It stated that power was becoming increasingly centralized in the national elites of third-world countries and in transnational corporations which escaped national regulations and transferred wealth from these countries to rich ones. The local elites in largely poor countries worked in alliance with international financial institutions such as the International Monetary Fund and the World Bank, it said, adding that policies which restricted government spending, devalued currencies and encouraged privatization had led to unemployment, lack of education, poverty and malnutrition — deprivations which, it noted, were especially felt by women and youth.

The report regretted that nature was treated solely as a resource input in the economic cycle, leading to resource depletion and environmental degradation. The "idols" of materialism, individualism and consumerism upheld the status quo and prevented real change, it said, while the "idol" of militarism drained resources, led to civil wars and paralyzed economies. Through the mass media, cultural identities had been transformed into the life-styles and values of those countries which controlled multinational corporations, the report said, and imposed a philosophy of life based on winners and losers, haves and have-nots, and of material value over human value.

The report called for a network of solidarity based on cooperation and equality, ideals which it said elude us in a free-market society. It emphasized the key role of education and called for the church to be a part of the struggle to achieve this. "We need to influence the church to increase its involvement in the community and the economy," it said. The report held that empowerment at the community level would lead to an increase in the value of human life rather than productivity or wealth, which had devastated many cultures and societies. "This vision will facilitate equality between genders, races and regions of the world," it added.

Of the two Bible study sessions at the gathering, one dealt with women's concerns, drawing from the support that Ruth and Naomi gave each other and received from Boaz, and the other with the environment, drawing upon the creation accounts in Genesis. If these two were the chief issues before the gathering, most of the forums had noted their relatedness. Indeed, if the gathering had a vision, it was not of a solution for the world's ills but of the inter-related nature of the problems they were grappling with. There was a perception, however vague, of a web of problems: of women, of the environment, of oppressed races, of education and economic systems, of poverty, of national debt, of fundamentalism, making of them all one complicated knot.

The gathering had little time, as it drew to an end, to put together the reports that they had produced in their different forums and to see the threads that united them, but the reports certainly seemed to add up to a unified message. Perhaps it is a failing of our analytical method of compartmentalized study that we so often don't see the possibilities to synthesize our analyses in such a way that we come up with a larger picture, one that might widen our horizons and give us a glimpse of the vision we seek. Once they are put together, though, and the strands that link them wound together, the reports present a remarkably unified picture of the basic problem facing the world and the ecumenical movement as the next century comes around.

3. Humanism Run Riot

As the world rethinks the ethics of consumption and development, perhaps Protestants have more cause for introspection than most others. It is the predominantly Protestant countries of northern Europe and North America that have the highest levels of consumption, the least remaining flora and non-human fauna, the most toxic pollutants, the highest rates of divorce and one-parent families and the most liberty for individualism of a sort that breeds alienation and social brokenness.

These are the peoples that have fought the most bloody wars, developed and used nuclear weapons, built their economies through colonial exploitation and race-based slavery, almost completely wiped out civilizations in North America and Australia and built apartheid in South Africa when they settled there.

It is these nations that are exporting debt, consumerism and the ethic of "market forces" to other parts of the world along with communication calculated to promote these earth-destroying values — values that are, fortunately, still alien to the majority of the world's peoples.

These nations and cultures surely need to address certain key questions: Has our quest for "a better life" led us to an essentially immoral sort of individualism? Has our search for greater and still greater wealth led us to rape the earth? Has our desire for liberty, humanist adventure and individual aspiration gone a little berserk?

Amid the onslaughts of pollution and environmental degradation that have marked the last quarter of the twentieth century, we need to look afresh at whether the European renaissance, the Protestant Reformation and the kind of unrestricted humanism that grew alongside both were good or bad — or perhaps a bit of both. Are the life-styles, worldviews and ethics which these engendered liberating, enabling and basically good? Or are they unsustainable, destructive and essentially immoral? Or are they, in fact, potentially either or even both, presenting us with a challenge to discover the optimal level of humanist liberty, a level that would not depend on the exploitation of other human beings and societies and would be sustainable for the earth?

There can be no doubt that the environment pays a price for humanism and that individual liberty flourishes at the expense of global equality. For human liberty stems from material wealth, which is accumulated through the deprivation of other peoples in other parts of the world and through the depredation of the earth. As more and more people across the globe are drawn swiftly into this individualist life-style, we need urgently to ask whether the earth has enough available for human consumption to sustain this kind of materially wealthy life-style if all the people of the world were to aspire to it, with plenty of choice for each one in every area of human activity.

Liberating potential

Humanism is not necessarily destructive. The space that humanist cultures have provided for individual liberty has allowed for liberation, particularly of women and younger persons. Another important argument in their favour is their generally democratic nature. The attitudes and aspirations they inculcate make for democratic sentiments and the members of these societies have a powerful say in how they are run and organized.

Quite clearly then, individual liberty is a positive value. As clearly, however, it can be disastrous if it is not harmonized with global equality and the integrity of nature. These three are like sides of a triangle, each of which must be balanced and the whole kept in harmony. During the twentieth century, individualism has been taken beyond sustainable limits to the extent that, if peoples in other parts of the world were to emulate the life-styles and behaviour patterns of these humanist, largely Protestant, societies, the impact of that much consumption on the earth would be not just unsustainable, it would be catastrophic.

24

Spiritual poverty

As practised in many of these societies, humanism and its concomitant individualism have led to material prosperity but also to spiritual bankruptcy. They have led to greater empirical knowledge than there had been before or elsewhere but broken all previous limitations on what was allowable for human beings. They have resulted in more completely developed and experienced individuals than before or elsewhere but have taken over all the space that other societies reserved as sacred for the rest of creation.

Most of these societies therefore have a large number of materially very wealthy people but also some materially poor people — apart from perhaps the world's most spiritually poor and lonely people and the most fractured societies in terms of families and relationships.

These cultures have snapped just about every link with nature, walling themselves in from it with concrete, asphalt and air-conditioning. The only animals they allow around them are either tamed and leashed or in zoos. Most of the plants they allow are ornamental or commercial in one way or another.

While these are not the only societies to have developed democratic norms or to have guaranteed enough space to the weak among them, they are perhaps the only cultures in the world to have exploited, enslaved and even exterminated other peoples in their quest for enough wealth to sustain their adventurism and greed.

Many of these often racist cultures have also contributed to great international injustice. For while humanism led to the end of feudal and class exploitation within these societies and to a certain level of gender equality, it also led to the physical, economic and cultural repression and exploitation of other peoples and nations on a global scale. It has also meant a debilitating cost to the parts of the earth which these societies have treated as resources for their industrialization and for their accumulation of material wealth.

Nor, generally, are these societies really egalitarian. Most of them are based on an ethic of competitiveness and treat the accumulation of material wealth as the most important measure of social success and honour. Those members who don't seek material wealth are treated as socially disabled, and losers get little by way of family and social support.

Essential restraints

The historical roots of this sort of culture go back to the Italian renaissance. The problem, however, could not be in the values and aspirations of the renaissance itself, for Italy's history and life-styles have not been as destructive as those of many of its neighbours to the north, to which the ideas and values of the renaissance spread.

It was in the countries where humanism and Protestantism, which unshackled another set of restraints, took firm root that these life-styles and attitudes flourished most. In the name of the "scientific temper", humanism shook off all the taboos which had, in various complex ways, restrained human beings from exploiting each other and the earth and all that is in it beyond certain limits.

Take, for instance, the song lines of the Australian Aboriginals. Entirely illogical and unscientific, these primitive tales which wound themselves around physical features of the land, the rivers, the animals and the plants among which the Aboriginal groups lived, prevented them from undertaking any sort of physical or economic activity that would desecrate the song lines only for their own material benefit. Through their belief in the song lines, they not only prevented themselves from developing wealthy life-styles but also from destroying nature, other plants and animals.

Many indigenous American, African and Asian societies worship the forests, rivers, mountains, or the ground around which they live. Some of them hold particular plants or animals as sacred. While such beliefs may seem unreasonable, they have certainly served to restrain these societies from defiling nature or exploiting it beyond a point. In fact, they have prevented these peoples from looking at the earth as a reservoir of resources which are meant to be used to increase the material wealth of these societies and the individuals in them.

Competitive ethic

Competition is the key to human behaviour in humanist societies and it too often blinkers people so that they can only see the road before them and the need to get ahead before the next person or the next family or the next country. The fear of getting left behind, of losing the race, blinds those who have turned humanism and individualism virtually into a modern religion to the sufferings of others and to the destructive effects of their endeavours on their environments.

It was as a result of that sort of competition between nations that Germans were roused to fascism and to the extermination of Jews and weaker peoples. They felt a sense of national humiliation at being left behind in Europe's race to colonize the world. The desire to eradicate from the face of the earth all those who were perceived to be weaker or inferior was a bizarre but logical culmination of the sort of scientific temper that sought to "improve" all things and to reach for "perfection" and a competitive edge, unmindful of the complex beauty and balance that pervades the apparent chaos in nature.

This sort of mindset sees all things — and people — in comparative terms, some being inferior to others, and as therefore needing "improvement". It has thus been able to justify black slavery, colonization and the exploitation of blacks and others in different parts of Africa, Latin America, Australia and Asia who were less competitive or ambitious than the humanist Europeans. If people were less competitive, it was presumed that this was because they were incapable of competing, and therefore inferior and in need of help to become more like the white humanists. That was the white man's burden during the horrible age of colonization.

This mindset is so blinkered by a collective conscious- ness of superiority and by each individual's fear of losing the race to get ahead of others, that it cannot see that the basic attitudes of most societies across the world are different and that they are not therefore necessarily back- ward or inferior. Most of the societies which this mindset has often looked down upon in fact live in some degree of harmony and integration with animals, plants and natural cycles.

Alternative development

Very many of them do not treat the accumulation of material possessions as the aim and driving inspiration for human lives. A lavish life-style with many material goods in the house is looked down upon as crass and greedy in many cultures. These cultures look up to austerity, sim- plicity, humility and quiet wisdom. Physical prowess is considered a lowly attribute while a disciplined, studious nature, a monastic or even mendicant life-style, is accorded great respect.

Some of these societies — most notably Japan — have achieved a degree of industrialization that allows for social equality. Indeed, Japan is one of the few nations that have achieved much material wealth for all its mem- bers while maintaining, at least to an extent, a culture of respect for nature and for simplicity, humility and wis- dom. Japan has a record of colonization but not of the sort of genocide Europeans have been guilty of. Nor is it as guilty of denuding the environment.

However, Japan is one of the few industrialized excep- tions among non-humanist societies. Much of the rest of

28

the world consists of agrarian economies. While these do not exploit other peoples and destroy the earth to the extent that humanist societies do, they are necessarily oppressive in structure. For the economic and material limitations of agrarian societies necessarily inhibit individual aspirations and deny the liberty to be equal members of society, particularly for women and youth.

Feudal repression

When the ruling elites of largely agrarian societies live materially wealthy life-styles, they generally build a highly repressive feudal society in which land is owned by the elite, who constitute a totally separate social class from the vast majorities of people who labour in the fields. The culture of these majorities must necessarily inhibit the liberty of individuals, particularly women and young people, and children. There isn't enough to sustain everybody's aspirations and so these majorities must labour hard to produce enough for their basic needs of food and clothing and to sustain the life-styles of the elite. They cannot be allowed to be "spoiled" by individual aspirations.

Most of these societies deny the majority of their members a democratic say in how they are run. Most of them thrive on socio-political systems that allow a small minority within them to exploit the vast majority. Individual liberty suffers in these societies as does the second side of the triangle that needs to be balanced: equality.

It is possible for these societies to become more egalitarian without becoming unsustainably rapacious with regard to their environments. More equality would automatically ensure more liberty and space and time for a more individually satisfying life-style for each member. The problem is that industrialization is essential to provide this and industrialization can easily set a society on the slippery slope towards a pattern of life that is unsustainable for the earth.

Fast change

Today, the life-styles, values and attitudes of the Protestant, humanist societies are being vigorously exported across the globe. More and more countries have been drawn into the ethic of competition and the mindset of unlimited growth — of material wealth. Instead of aspiring to production levels and life-styles that would make for equality and be sustainable for their environments, their often nascent industries try to compete with more advanced industrial societies, making the economically poorer people of these hitherto simpler societies undertake industrial labour in a soul-destroying work cycle, often in poorly ventilated sweat shops. Learning nothing from history, they go through the same processes which European societies went through a century or so ago, in which spirituality and the human spirit are as much a victim as the earth and its natural wealth.

The education systems of these societies change and, often through Christian missions, the ethic of competition, of struggling to be first in class rather than to understand basic truths, becomes the criterion of success at school. Not only in trade, industry and agricultural production but also through such events as the Olympics, the ethic of being faster, higher and stronger as being better is actively promoted. The ethic of harmony, fraternity and tolerance falls by the wayside.

Mass communication media project and popularize this sort of ethic and life-style through soap operas and such programmes as MTV. It is as if all human beings and societies were being pushed into one gigantic race with each other in the name of "progress" to become more and more competitive, assertive and acquisitive.

4. Nations in Ferment

By the end of the 1980s and into the 1990s, the concept of nationhood became ill-defined and confusing in an increasing number of places across the globe. From Bosnia to Afghanistan, Europe to South Africa, Palestine to Fiji, established nations were under severe pressure as peoples sought to redefine themselves. Ethnic divisions were frequently complicated by religious tensions and religious fundamentalism took firm hold on the minds of people in many countries.

As young people grew up in the last two decades of the twentieth century and came to grips with the world around them, they lacked the assurance of an established political geography. All around them, nations appeared to be in ferment, changing their boundaries, breaking up, uniting, or forming huge alliances. Some of them weren't clear about which way they were going as different sections of people made contradictory claims about their nationhood. In many cases, conflicts were violently engaged.

The most important and dramatic change, of course, was the break-up of the Soviet Union, which just a decade earlier had seemed like a mighty, unshakeable monolith. The speed with which it crumbled provided an impetus to latent fissiparous tendencies in other countries, most notably in Yugoslavia. The respect which the Soviet Union had given to plurality resulted in a relatively peaceful separation. Tito's imposition of a unitary culture in Yugoslavia had obviously created much deeper resentments and among the nations that emerged from the break-up there have been savage conflicts.

Such savagery was not limited to Serbia and Bosnia. Sri Lanka, Rwanda and Angola are only some of the countries where ethnic conflicts were terribly bloody as ethnic groups sought to decimate those they saw as their rivals and as posing a threat to their social and economic progress or even to their existence. In some places, this ethnicity was defined in terms of tribes, in others as races.

Very often, differences of religion overlapped these divisions. In Sri Lanka, the ethnic Tamils are generally Hindu, the ethnic Sinhalas mainly Buddhist. In Ireland, of course, the battle lines are drawn primarily on the basis of confessional loyalties.

In other countries, which may have remained calm on the surface, ethnic tensions of one kind or another exist but without having assumed violent proportions — at least as yet. In the US, for instance, the tensions between blacks and others became dramatically obvious during the Los Angeles riots in 1992. Aboriginals in Australia and indigenous peoples in many countries of America chafe at their exploitation over the past few centuries. In Chiapas province of Mexico, such tensions boiled over in early 1994.

If yesterday's generation sought ways to live peaceably as nations and with other nations, there is an urgent need among today's generation to discover the essentials necessary for nations to live in peace and harmony, not only with others but also within themselves. There can be no simple formula, because different parts of the world are being swept by vastly different currents of history.

Different currents
While the two major changes of the age — in Western Europe and the former Soviet Union — are dictated by the economic interests of industrially developed countries, those in many parts of Africa and Asia are generally the processes of transition from agrarian, feudal socio-political systems to competitive, industrial ones.

The basic pattern of these latter conflicts is that one or another ethnic group dominates political and economic power, leading to reactions, sometimes violent, from those who feel they're unfairly treated. The Soviet Union fits this pattern. Western Europe does not. In a sense, the break-up of the Soviet Union complements the integration of Western Europe, as the pivot of power on that continent shifts. Significantly, the first among the Soviet nations to try and break away were the Baltic republics, which were eager to join the tide of Western European integration.

Western Europe meanwhile is shedding the inhibitions of ethnic nationalism as it seeks to build a powerful economic partnership that could challenge the economic might of the US and Japan. Western Europe, where modern nationalism first took root, is thus in a post-nationalist phase of history now while most other parts of the world are consolidating or coming to terms with nationalism — often with great difficulty.

European nationalism

Modern nationalism first grew in Europe through the period after the renaissance. Its democratic systems, its legal traditions and its separation of church and state grew organically out of the attitudes and social patterns engendered by renaissance humanism and its concomitant individualism and attachment to liberty. Most other parts of the world retained social and political patterns that were based on less ambitious and assertive life-styles and traditions.

Through these centuries, most Europeans came to view Europe as the centre of the world and all other continents as appendages — only to be conquered and used. Their ethnic nationalism became intensely competitive — the way some other parts of the world are now becoming — until the nations within it fought two wars which involved practically the whole world, during the first half of this century. Until then, the European nations had managed to keep much of the rest of the world colonized. Consequently, older traditions of nationhood withered in some of these places.

After the two world wars debilitated the European nations, the new super-nations — the Soviet Union and the US — took the lead in world dominance, squeezing Europe between them. Even a nation like Japan, which had been defeated in the second world war, became economically more powerful than any of the European nations within a few decades of that war.

During the four decades after the second world war, the delicate balance of power between the US and the USSR ensured that one or the other of them exerted a powerful influence over almost every other part of the world. Latent tensions and conflicts in many of the nascent nations were kept under control by one or the other of these two powers. Amid the collapse of the USSR and the ensuing confusion in global relationships, many of these tensions boiled over during the late 1980s and early 1990s.

Religious strife

It is interesting that the former Czechoslovakia split so painlessly while the former Yugoslavia disintegrated into such a horribly violent conflict. Could it have to do with the fact that the ethnic differences in Yugoslavia were reinforced by differences in religion? The violence there is inspired by the kind of hatred that Northern Ireland has witnessed for a century of Protestant-Roman Catholic conflict. It is the same sort of mindless violence and hatred that accompanied the formation of India and Pakistan in 1947. Here, the differences were not ethnic at all. The separation was entirely based on religion. The hatred lingers on even today, more than half a century after the partition of the sub-continent. The bitterly violent conflict in Sri Lanka too is between ethnic groups which are divided by religion.

Is it because religion was not a separating factor in the race-based apartheid that South Africans were able so peacefully and easily to put the past behind them, despite the unbelievable oppression and humiliation which the

whites had heaped on the blacks and other "coloured"
people of the country during those many decades?

Is it because religion is an element in the Israel-
Palestine conflict that the peace efforts there went through
so much more difficulty than the dismantling of apartheid,
which had appeared until the mid-1980s to be a far more
intractable and potentially violent problem?

It does seem as if religion, when it becomes an
element in ethnic conflicts or even conflicts within otherwise homogeneous communities, leads to much greater
hatred and fear of the other group and therefore to great
brutality.

Fundamentalist reactions

Fundamentalism is a different phenomenon, not so
much a manifestation of inter-religious competition as a
reaction against alien life-styles, non-traditional social and
political concepts. Islamic fundamentalism in particular,
and Hindu fundamentalism too, are at least partly a reaction
against the social dislocation that swift industrialization
causes. Iran under Shah Reza Pahlavi, for instance, sought
to become economically and socially Westernized very
fast, faster than the common people were prepared for.
Since there were no democratic institutions through which
people could resist the pace of change, they flocked to the
reassuring traditionalism of Ayatollah Khomeini.

The humanism and individualism which the renaissance spawned and Protestantism bred provided the
philosophical undergirding for Europeans a few centuries
ago to break out of the security of the feudal, tightly-knit
social structures that bind every agrarian society. Without
a renaissance attitude, other nations often revolt against
the social consequences of an industrialization process
that blindly imposes humanist ideas and systems.

The modern concepts of nationalism, democracy, the
nation-state and its institutions have often been imposed

by puppet regimes or elites educated by the North who do not have any clear understanding of local urges. They have been imposed without an adequate process of organic social, cultural and political transformation to prepare these peoples for the new, alien institutions.

These modern, democratic institutions are suited to individualist attitudes and social mores and depend on the strict exclusion of often restrictive religious hierarchies from political processes. But many of these societies are steeped in traditions or even political systems that give religious leaders a major say in secular affairs. They are also used to feudal social patterns in which community leaders dominate and others obey largely without question. Very often, they identify themselves as ethnic groups rather than as individuals and fear the dominance of one or another ethnic group on the levers of administration in their nascent or young nations.

Most of these cultures across the world are revolted by the sort of humanism that entails disrespect for other animals and for the earth and all that is in it, that allows the unbridled freedom of the individual at the cost of family, tribe, village or nation. The culture that Western multinational companies, and the advertising and media programming which accompany them, take into these more integrated cultures causes strong reactions and often strengthens fundamentalists who lead campaigns against what they perceive as an assault on their values, cultures and, by extension, their religion.

New industrialization
The clash of humanist and feudal values is not the only cause for conflict, of course. Many of the conflicts in the countries of Asia and Africa are rooted in economic impoverishment. When there isn't enough to go around, there is bound to be a fight over the little there is. Unfair trading systems, the purchase of industrial raw materials

at prices that are often controlled by industrialized and politically powerful purchasers and the burden of national debt all lead to situations in which agricultural prices in essentially agrarian economies fall to the extent that agriculture for food production becomes unviable. That leads to famine, shortages and therefore to violence, disruption and large-scale migrations of refugees.

Part of the reason for the rash of conflicts in recent years is the skewered way in which many nations are making the transition from an agrarian economy to an industrial one, too often without adequate capital to set up industry or the technology to run it, without the money to import capital, technology or raw materials, or markets to export their products to.

Industry requires movement of goods and workers and leads to a greater feeling of nationalism among the common people than they would normally have had when they were an agrarian society. With industrialization, their horizons expand both in terms of movement from one place to another within their countries and in terms of the comforts they aspire to possess. Their aspirations and their needs increase. With that their pride in nationhood and their sense of competition — with other nations as well as with other communities, ethnic or religious, within their nations — also increase. Lacking capital, technology and markets, however, the industrial growth of these nations is inevitably too sluggish to match the aspirations of the people for a better life-style. The consequent sense of frustration is easily channelled into the sense of competition with other groups and leads to conflict with those communities that are perceived to have cornered more than their share.

Many newly industrializing societies have accepted more or less autocratic rulers in exchange for stability as they grapple with their seemingly insoluble economic problems. These despots, sometimes religious fundamentalists, provide some measure of the feudal security systems which these hitherto agrarian societies have been used to. They also guarantee, by use of force, that ethnic and communal conflicts are kept in check.

Agrarian societies

As long as people live in agrarian economies, their world is largely restricted to the village and their needs to the produce of the village and the nearest town. They may be part of huge empires but ordinary village people in such traditional agrarian societies have little concept of or interest in a larger political entity than their immediate village and the nearest town or city.

An agrarian society is almost always ordered in a feudal hierarchy and only the ruling class can aspire to anything like a humanist life-style. Non-agricultural production is largely limited to handicrafts and art, and there is not enough of what may broadly be called comforts for everyone to possess. Nor do traditional agricultural incomes allow for such purchases.

There is little concept of nationalism. A section of the village may be dedicated to a feudal master or a king as a volunteer force to be called up when his territory is invaded or he wants to enlarge his territory. The village normally pays a tax, generally to a feudal lord appointed for the purpose by the king. The common people generally accept, often under religious instruction, that the inequality of the feudal class structure is established by God.

Hunting societies

Until the twentieth century, most of the world outside Europe and the nations that emerged through the migration of Europeans to other continents remained in either such agrarian economies and feudal political structures or in hunting and food-gathering societies, which were even less a part of a larger political entity and whose members had no sense of nationhood at all beyond their immediate communities. These food-gathering societies normally recognized no feudal or political authority outside the tribe or village. Their needs were even smaller than those of settled agrarian societies, their respect for the earth greater.

Such hunting societies were the norm in large parts of Africa and in the Americas and the Pacific islands before European settlers got to these places. They also lived, particularly in forest tracts, in the midst of settled agrarian societies in many parts of Asia.

Their wants were minimal and most of them lived in harmony with the earth and her bounties. Some of them worshipped the earth, the mountains, the rivers, the trees. What industrialized societies call the environment was safe from them.

Colonial legacies

Europeans passed on their notions of modern nationhood to the largely agrarian or food-gathering societies which they dominated during the past few centuries. Alongside, they built such features of industrialized society as communication and transport networks and set up mining and other basic industries that could supply raw materials to the industries in their home countries. To staff these and to help them to run these countries, they created elites among the peoples they ruled.

These elites picked up European concepts of nationhood and humanism, were consequently inspired to struggle for independence from the colonizers and sought to set up nations cast in the European mould when they won independence. Often, the colonizers had patronized or used a particular tribe, caste or other ethnic group to build the elite which helped them rule, and this community tended to control the political and economic levers of the new nation. As other communities chafed under the dominance of this community, ethnic and tribal conflicts emerged in a very large number of these countries in Asia and Africa towards the end of the twentieth century.

In Sri Lanka, for instance, the ethnic Tamils were often more educated than the numerically dominant Sinhalas and dominated government jobs during Britain's rule. After independence in 1948, the Sinhalas sought to reverse the imbalance by reserving jobs, and seats in educational institutions. The Tamils revolted and demanded a separate state for themselves. The Sinhalas refused and Sri Lanka has become the stage, since 1983, for one of the most bitter and violent ethnic conflicts in the world.

During the 1980s, more and more communities of those who used to be hunters and food-gatherers have begun to come to grips with what has been done to their cultures and life-styles, their lands and their heritage. They have now identified themselves as the original or indigenous peoples of various lands across the earth and agitate against the way they have been exploited and marginalized in the nations that have emerged around them, many of which have taken over their traditional lands by force or deception. Few of them have had the strength, numerical or economic, to engage in violent conflict but their cry is a major challenge to nations across the world. Many of these communities want the space to be able to continue their simple life-styles, close to nature and in harmony with all creation.

Modern conundrum

While it is difficult to respond to the complaints of these hunting societies, there can be no denying that the industrialization that has accompanied modern national-ism in almost all countries across the world over the latter half of the twentieth century has brought more social and gender equality to agrarian societies. Particularly where nationalism has been accompanied by genuine democratic structures, it has broken or diluted the feudal structures which were the norm in agrarian societies far more than in the generally more egalitarian food-gathering societies.

Feudal societies in many parts of the world were built on one form of slavery or another, whether the system was known as caste, serfdom or bonded or plantation labour. The minority elites who owned land dominated the societies around them, imposing their whims and often exploiting women. Women in fact suffered the triple burden of being in physical danger from the men of the privileged class, of contributing their labour to add to the household income, and of having to manage and hold together their families even when the men who dominated them were irresponsible or violent.

The urbanization and individualism which accompany industrialization lead, in combination with the notion of nationalism, to breaking down the divisions of class, race and other forms of discrimination. Workers in large cities, away from the narrow confines of their village roots and educated to identify themselves as citizens of the nation rather than as members of their ethnic communities, are far more likely to marry outside their communities than their forefathers. Industrial urbanization and individualism, then, would seem to be a gradual antidote to ethnic conflict.

This, of course, means a change of attitudes and ideas, essentially an adoption of some measure of humanism and individualism. Yet, as long as there isn't enough to go around, nationalism and individualism can only lead to exacerbating ethnic tensions and violent conflicts, for they inevitably unleash aspirations for life-styles and possessions that are difficult to realize. These aspirations and the industry which accompanies them also, of course, do great damage to the earth and all that is in it.

The conundrum of our times is to ensure that all people get the advantages of industrialization, urbanization and consumption that modern nation-states can provide, but get these without being trapped by the individualist greed and frustrations that lead to conflict. The challenge is to find the optimal level of industrialization and consumption, the right balance between modern individualism and traditional ethnicity, between competitive nationalism and traditional community spirit. All nations, those that have more than this level and those that have less, must gradually aspire to this optimum. This balance is essential not only for the integrity of the earth and all creation but also for peace among nations and peoples.

5. Explosive Growth

In the last quarter of the twentieth century, young people have been bombarded with bad news about two global problems: the debt crisis and the threat to the environment.

They have heard of nations going bankrupt, of national debts that have mortgaged the lives of generations yet unborn, of spiralling inflation rates that have taken even basic necessities out of the reach of many hard-working people, of recessions that put trained men and women out of employment.

They have heard of thousands dying of starvation as the agricultural economies of nations crumble before the lure of cash crops or before the dumping of highly subsidized agricultural products. They have heard of the manipulation of agricultural prices by those who have the power to influence world trade.

They have heard of entire island nations beginning to disappear as the oceans rise because of global warming, of the hole in the ozone layer that is letting lethal sunrays into the earth's atmosphere, of endangered species and threatened rain forests.

These crises are the bequest of those, mainly in the materialistic and individualistic North, who, particularly over the past century, have treated the earth and the peoples of some parts of the world as objects for enjoyment, as resources for their advancement and glorification, unconcerned about the effects of their wasteful life-styles on others, on the earth, and on their own great-grandchildren.

As the world shies away from these complex and apparently intractable problems, things are getting worse every day. Powerful policy-makers refuse to correlate the problems of the environment with the problems of national economies. Even as they see that the earth is sending signal after signal that it cannot take any more human profligacy, that its life-sustaining ecosystems are breaking down under the assaults of more and more human consumption, economists prescribe faster economic growth around the world, growth that will require the destruction of more of the earth and all that is in it for the production of goods for human consumption, growth that will produce more toxic wastes and industrial effluents to pollute the earth, its rivers, its soils and, perhaps now, even its oceans.

Hardly any policy-maker seems willing to realize, or at least to take the stand, that consumption must decrease, that some human life-styles must become less comfortable and that some economies must shrink if the earth, the environment in which human beings live, is to survive the way we know it. It almost seems as if we have become a collective ostrich, hoping that the earth will somehow stop crumbling if we bury our head in the sands of growth long enough.

Media control

One reason nobody talks about this destructive spiral of growth, or the limits to the sustainable expansion of industrial production and human consumption, is that discussion is controlled by the mass media, which are today designed primarily as vehicles for advertising. The great boast of an advertising man is that he can sell ice to Eskimos. Very funny, but he means it. His profession is not about what people need. It's all about expanding markets, selling more, which means producing more, which means destroying more — all for no better reason than that it's still possible for economies to grow.

Even a generation ago, newspapers thought of themselves as practising the profession of communicating news and ideas, often with an intellectual commitment to particular ideologies or political and economic systems. Over the past decade or so, they have been overshadowed by television as purveyors of news, and television has rarely ever thought of itself as anything other than a business to earn revenue by pulling in advertisements — by getting and keeping entertained as many viewers as possible of the sort that advertisers want to reach. In many countries which had a long tradition of intellectually rigorous news-paper journalism, newspapers have, as they fight off competition from television, begun to view themselves the same way as many television companies do, as vehicles for advertisements.

Activist groups have taken up environmental concerns vigorously since the 1970s, but most of them have con-centrated on efforts to conserve particular species of animals or plants, or on certain ecosystems or life-styles. Most of them have not come to grips with the larger trends of human development, attitudes and life-styles. Individu-als in industrialized societies who are concerned about the degradation of the environment may consume less than the average in their consumption-oriented communities, yet they still perhaps consume more than would be sustainable for the earth if each single human being in the world was to live a life-style similar to theirs, consume as much and create as much non-biodegradable waste.

Sustainable societies

The fact is that — though the proportion is fast chang-ing with the rapid recent growth of Asian economies — more than half of the world's population of human beings still maintain life-styles that are sustainable for the earth. Many of those who are bred on humanism look upon these peoples as poor simply because they consume less than humanists. Yet, many of them consume enough to live healthy lives long enough to raise their children to adult-hood so that they can continue the cycle of procreation.

Their lives are limited largely to their villages and nearby towns, but so are their needs. Since aspirations are limited and there is little scope for loneliness, alienation or stress, social norms are generally accepted and followed and crime is therefore restricted. Societies are closely-knit and people find happiness in small pleasures, often in celebrations of nature and her gifts.

By no means are these societies idyllic, though — at least for the weak among them. They are often restrictive, particularly for women, the young and those who have no control over land — mainly because food is limited and they must work hard together to grow or hunt it. Since they depend on nature for their agricultural inputs, they sometimes face famines and have few defences against floods and other natural calamities.

Worse, these societies often have some class, caste or other form of social oppression, primarily again because there isn't enough to go around and the dominant classes or ethnic groups corner the best, sometimes subjecting powerless classes to callous treatment. These underclasses are often gradually malnourished. Women of these underclasses bear the brunt of double exploitation, from the men and elders of their families and the men and women of the upper classes.

The greater availability of goods and money that comes with industrialization has made for social equality, between races, classes and genders, in various parts of the world. For, through efficient technologies, economies of scale and competition, big industries reduce the prices of goods to bring them within the reach of even the economically poorer classes in a society. They thus contribute to building more egalitarian societies, often freeing women from the laborious traditional processes of cooking and running homes. If they provide jobs, they also provide these classes with the money to buy their goods.

Going too far

However, advertising then goes on to create and accentuate social distinctions with its concept of niche marketing for what it terms the upmarket and the mass market. Upmarket goods are generally things that people would never have thought they needed until advertising convinced them it was fashionable.

As a society becomes affluent, everyone starts to want the delicacies and fine arts that were the exclusive preserve of a small elite of the preceding feudal society. When everyone wants to have a hunting holiday the way the aristocracy used to, many species of animals get wiped out. So also, when everyone wants a share of whale's or snake's meat. The Chinese government has had to appeal to Chinese citizens not to consume so many snakes as to threaten the reptiles with extinction.

The challenge before this generation of youth, then, is to seek models of economic growth that would allow for inequitable societies to industrialize adequately to make for equality and justice within them without setting them on a path of hedonistic acquisitiveness for goods, which would gradually make their life-styles unsustainable for the earth, tear the fabric of their social relationships to shreds and alienate soulless individualists from others to the extent that they do not even bat an eyelid when another human being is murdered in front of them on a city street.

Communist failures

Through most of the twentieth century, many intellectuals and oppressed people looked to communism as a system for industrialization that provided comprehensive controls on the greed of human beings. It seemed to guarantee social and economic equality, adequate food, clothing, housing and other human needs, to control crime and other deviations from social norms, and not to allow wasteful consumption.

By the last decade of the century, though, the system had been discredited. The most outstanding communist experiment, the Soviet Union, had collapsed, taking down with it a large number of other European communist systems. The Soviet Union's industry has been exposed as chaotic, producing goods for which there is no demand and not enough of what is required.

Wherever it was tried, though most notably in places like Romania, the system bred corruption and nepotism, and therefore inequality. While the party cadre who ran things could effectively control the greed of the common people, it is now evident that the greed and nepotism of such a cadre itself gradually and inevitably eats into the vitals of the system.

Communist regimes inevitably seem to become dictatorships, often centred around the glorification of one individual "great leader". Elections are generally reduced to processes of automatically placing a stamp of approval on candidates chosen by the supreme arbiter or those he trusts in the communist cadre. To secure his position, he has to allow this cadre the leeway for the nepotism and corruption which undermine the system.

Nor does anyone get to know what is happening. Whatever the faults of the big media empires of today's world, they have exposed the misdoings of those in power, even forcing the resignation of President Richard Nixon in the US. While some of the media in a society may be biased one way or another, freedom and competition between media organizations allow people to choose which source of information they want to trust. They certainly get to know what's happening from one or another of the newspapers or radio or television stations.

Democracy has its drawbacks, such as the high recurrent expense of elections, including the waste of trees for paper to print posters, flags, pamphlets and ballots, but there appears to be a consensus among the majority of young people at the end of the twentieth century that democracy is preferable to any other system of choosing a government.

48

Frustrated aspirations

There is a more basic drawback to any communist
state that accepts humanist principles. The wide education
and the sophisticated communication and transport technologies of an industrial society inevitably create aspirations among people who, a generation or two earlier in
agrarian milieus, might never have thought of travelling
more than fifty kilometres from their homes all their lives
or of possessing anything that was not produced within
five hundred. Cultures in such milieus would generally
subordinate individual aspirations to the welfare and needs
of the community. By promoting humanist principles and
providing people with the material goods essential for a
humanist life-style but forcibly denying them opportunities to fulfil the consequent aspirations for more,
communism alienates people and removes from their lives
the motivation to work.

It is dangerous to create a hiatus between supply and
demand, for that inevitably leads to frustration. Greed and
waste must be controlled through persuasion, education
and, most important, the philosophies that determine
people's attitudes.

Prohibiting a sense of ownership and belonging is also
no way to curb greed. In communist agriculture, the
concept of community or state ownership removes the
motivation which a sense of individual or family ownership provides for people to work hard and to produce
more. Once the managers of the system become corrupt,
the production process can easily break down, leading to
shortages and to economic chaos.

Ownership doesn't only signify a profit motive. Many
farmers in agrarian economies produce little more than
their own families can consume. Yet they work hard to
produce the best they can from their little farms. What
communist systems have often failed to realize is the
importance for human beings of a sense of ownership, of

partnership, of attachment, of responsibility, of creativity, of achievement, of satisfaction. It is possible to turn a human society into a vast machine, each member performing an assigned task with discipline, but the cogs in that machine soon begin to lose the resilience that is the hallmark of human beings.

Wasteful life-styles

For all their failings, communist societies have been an advantage to the earth for they have discouraged extravagant life-styles and wasteful consumption. That, unfortunately, is exactly the kind of life-style that has been promoted the world over in place of the failing communist economies since the late 1980s and as an antidote to the faltering welfare states and the transient economies that have been caught in foreign-debt traps since the 1970s. Forced to turn to the World Bank and the International Monetary Fund, these cash-strapped countries have had to accept a free-market model of economic growth along with drastic cuts in governmental welfare spending and low tariffs, essentially to enable multinational industrial giants to market their products freely among their people.

A classic free-market model based on the supply of goods produced in response to the demand expressed in terms of people's needs is fine, but multinationals and other large industries have a clear agenda: to expand markets by creating desires where there is no need through advertising and the media. This has two devastating effects. It destroys the earth, other animals, plants and all else that is in the earth, to produce goods that nobody really needs. And it creates such unhealthy levels of desire for goods that families and societies begin to come apart.

Until the 1950s or the 1960s, Western industry was production-driven, as it sought to produce goods to meet people's needs. Thereafter, Western industry has swiftly changed to become marketing-driven, seeking to create desires for goods which people would otherwise have felt no need for. The unnecessary production of these goods uses up so much more of the earth and what is in it when the earth is already collapsing under the weight of so much human consumption.

On the other hand, increasingly mechanized and computerized technologies have meant that, by the 1980s and the 1990s, many huge plants require barely any labour at all. The result is that large sections of the population become unemployed, unable to make ends meet and certainly not to satisfy the aspirations that advertisements generate. Frustration leads to crime and to the collapse of social networks of support and even of families. The sordid lives of the street children of Rio de Janeiro are only the tip of the iceberg of social rot that an industrial economy derailed can cause.

Another effect of mechanization in factories is that an ever-larger proportion of industry is in services, offering an ever-expanding host of comforts, holidays and life-style alternatives — as far as possible, upmarket ones. These services may help to take care of the employment problem but create ever more profligate life-styles and aspirations, which result in the destruction of more and more of the earth and all that is in it.

The aspiration for these services fuels more frustration among those who cannot afford them, increasing crime and the further breakdown of families. Those that can find work sometimes take on two or even more jobs, neglecting their children as they run faster and faster, chasing the rainbow.

Obviously, different parts of the world and different socio-economic classes within societies need to aspire and move in different directions today. Large parts of the world, particularly in Africa and Asia, need industrial growth to the extent that each member of each society can have basic comforts, and underclasses, women and younger persons can be liberated from their inequitable, often feudal, agrarian societies.

At the same time, large sections of the populations of many North American, European and some Asian countries must not only limit their aspirations but start working towards building economic systems and life-styles that make for much decreased consumption. There is no time to lose for, as the other half — or perhaps three-fourths — increases consumption, the earth is going to move faster than ever before towards breaking point. The burden on her must be eased.

6. Destructive Attitudes

Some years ago, I told a friend in Switzerland that he must visit me in India. He said no, that would be immoral. He believed that people should depend for their needs on what was available around where they lived and was against the import and export of goods for human consumption across the globe. He disapproved of heavy industry and of life-styles that necessitated such levels of industrialization. He felt people should seek contentment in fulfilling their essential needs and his own life-style conformed to this. Naturally, then, he would not travel on an airplane, certainly not to go halfway across the globe just for the enjoyment of seeing an exotic part of the world.

He was one of the most contented persons I have known. Despite having been born in the centre of modern, humanist Europe, he pursued happiness in caring quietly for those around him rather than in fulfilling personal desires and seeking individual enrichment. Many, many young people seem to be looking for such contentment at the end of the twentieth century but feel trapped in a mindset that one must fulfil oneself with experiences, enjoyment and consumption. Travel, leisure, dressing, eating, drinking, everything is promoted as part of the pursuit of happiness — promoted by advertising and the media as well as by modern education systems.

There are two dimensions to this problem. One is that industrialization has gone berserk over the course of this century, developing an apparently unstoppable momentum towards exponentially increasing production, in terms of both volume and types of goods, without any relevance to the needs of people. The second dimension is the way human beings view themselves, their importance and the importance of their achieving success, happiness and fulfilment. That too has gone berserk and people in some societies have a sense of their individual importance that would be funny were it not also so pathetic and dangerous for the earth and other creatures.

That is perhaps why, during the very decades from the 1960s onwards when many Western societies liberalized their folk cultures to shake off all taboos, many young people in these societies turned to Buddhism, Hinduism and other Eastern traditions that have always stressed equanimity, tranquillity and harmony, rather than humanism and individualism.

Consumerist disappointments

It has been a period of great social trauma in these Western societies. What is more dangerous is that the onward sweep of the consumerist industrial culture which multinational companies have been leading more and more vigorously into countries of the South since the 1970s is trying to trap young people in these societies too in the same sort of mindset.

Since this consumerist culture thrives on advertisement promises — of fulfilment, enjoyment, satisfaction, accomplishment — and on promoting desires for all manner of goods and experiences, it leads often to frustration among young persons — either because of disappointment after consumption or because of the inability to obtain what is advertised. Both kinds of frustration lead to violence, anger and recrimination.

The confused young victims generally hold their parents and society at large responsible for their disappointments and, as parents struggle to cope with their own frustrations, family life becomes more and more strained. Sadly, it is in societies where resources are most scarce that the potential for frustration and recrimination is greatest. Social and moral norms that have been respected for centuries fall by the wayside and societies begin to accept sex tourism, as in parts of Thailand, or turn to street violence, as in Brazil's cities.

When the pursuit of happiness becomes the pursuit of fads, goods and experiences for individual enrichment, and individuals think their satisfaction is desperately important, social networks of support and care break down. Older persons in various parts of the world have probably never before been as sad as in the latter half of the twentieth century, as children and other younger family members have shaken off traditions of living with and caring for them.

Children likewise have never before had such lonely childhoods, sometimes deserted or ignored by one or both parents. Nursing, tending and feeding progeny, which most animals treat as one of their central roles in life, has increasingly tended to be viewed in many societies in recent decades as an imposition, an irksome task that interferes with the pursuit of individual enrichment and the enjoyment of life.

Families have tended to break up as more and more individualists have refused to make compromises and to subordinate their individual aspirations to the need for unity and harmony among family members. Consequently, divorce has almost become the norm in some societies. This is of course partly an inevitable result of the pressures and tensions of the fast-paced working lives of an industrial society but it also has much to do with the mindset of modern men and women, the great importance they attach to their individual selves and the fulfilment of their desires.

Japanese alternative

Not all societies are set in this mould, though. Many Asian societies, some of them rooted in Buddhism or Hinduism, have maintained a self-effacing sort of culture that frowns upon self-assertion even in casual conversations, and demands conformity to rituals such as bowing that constantly show respect for others. Some of them practise ancestor worship and show elaborate respect for older family members. There is often great societal pressure for tending children and for at least one parent to spend a lot of time with them. Social bonds may sometimes become cloying but they generally prevent the sort of alienation, psychological disorientation and loneliness that is virtually endemic in some Northern societies.

The Japanese have demonstrated that it is quite possible to be highly industrialized and yet not have to assert individuality, to develop and produce a large range of goods without creating an advertising-driven culture of indiscriminate consumption. In fact, Western advertising professionals often wonder at how Japanese advertisements, which they view as slow and dull, ever manage to sell anything, but they do. That's the sort of image that Japanese culture responds to.

Japanese products have tended to cater to a more egalitarian society than those of the US or Europe, producing high quality for everyone rather than upmarket goods meant exclusively for those who can spend more within a society. Japanese cars naturally came to dominate the world market during the time when the limits on the earth's capacity to provide oil began to be widely perceived. They were fuel-efficient, high-performance cars that looked smart and were reasonably large. Plus they were affordable for the middle classes. Western upmarket models, on the other hand, generally consumed much more fuel and were designed to generate envy. They were not only generally oblivious to the need to conserve the earth's depleting oil wealth, they were bound to create social tensions. The big US cars of the 1950s and 1960s were in fact designed to flaunt a life-style of absolute abandonment to enjoyment. They were the ultimate statement of the ethic of individualism, the unbridled pursuit of happiness.

Although they live in one of the most industrialized societies in the world, the Japanese generally do not simply aspire to everything that other societies have. In most Japanese homes, people sit on the floor in traditional style. They have not unnecessarily adopted chairs, which consume so much wood, as many societies elsewhere in Asia, which also once used mats or carpets, have done. Chairs were originally necessary in a utilitarian sense only in very cold climates, particularly among those societies which had not developed the art of making woolen or silk carpets the way the inhabitants of the Pamir and Himalayan mountains had done.

Unlike many other Asian and African societies, the Japanese have resisted individualism. The pursuit of individual career goals is discouraged in Japan if it does not conform to the larger good of all those who work in a firm or factory. The larger social good is placed squarely above that of the individual who wants to get ahead of the pack. Yet, the employment norms through which this is done do not smother the motivation to work hard and produce efficiently, as communist norms too often do.

Japanese society is not ideal, though. The pressures on women are immense and the high incidence of suicide in contemporary Japan indicates that coping with the dual pressures of achieving in a highly industrial economy and maintaining the requirements of a self-effacing culture can take a heavy toll.

The challenge before the generation that will live most of their lives in the twenty-first century is to discover the right balance between individualism and self-effacement in order to accommodate others in one's immediate society without being oppressed by them.

Danger of passivity

A certain amount of individualist assertiveness is essential to guard against oppression. A number of essentially feudal societies repress the majority of their members in the name of maintaining traditions. Women, younger persons and certain races, tribes or castes are unjustly repressed in very many parts of the world, and not only in feudal societies. The difference is that, when this happens in humanist, individualist societies, these values allow — even empower — the oppressed to resist and struggle for change more easily than they could in other societies.

A mindset that shuts out virtually any individual aspiration, a mindset of bovine indifference to the injustices around one — which some of the economically less-developed, feudal societies generate — can be as dangerous as a highly individualist mindset. It is this sort of passive mindset that allows powerful elites to manipulate situations that force millions of people, with barely any resources or goods, to flee their homes as refugees, as in Rwanda in 1994 and in Bangladesh in 1971.

Mahatma Gandhi sought to give India a balanced sort of attitude to social responsibility. He wanted a society that was highly aware, and dedicated to providing justice and equality to all, but was not acquisitive or individualist. He backed "high thinking, simple living" and recommended non-violent "satyagraha", which means search for truth, struggle against every kind of oppression.

He had taken over, in the second decade of the twentieth century, the leadership of a movement which had grown until then among the small minority of Indians who had shaken off — either under European influence or through the nineteenth-century Hindu religious and cultural reform movements — the mindset of indifference and complete acceptance, even of injustice. While marrying the movements for political independence and social reform, Gandhi promoted an austere life-style, one of tolerance, absolute non-violence and the consumption of only what was available around one. Towards this last end, he encouraged each person to weave his or her own clothes. To achieve self-control and self-abnegation, he advocated abstinence from sex over periods of time.

India has gradually rejected the Gandhian ideal over the decades since his assassination but his is the sort of attitude to life and to self that the generation which is looking for a suitable life-style for the new century perhaps needs.

7. After the Peak

The trend towards individualism which began with the European renaissance six centuries ago reached a peak in the 1960s. Young people and students in almost all those societies across the globe which had been influenced by humanism and were not controlled under communist dictatorships participated in what some of them called a revolution. They broke many taboos, railed against "the system" and rebelled against all the social, cultural, religious and sartorial traditions they could. Many of them gave free rein to their desires, let their hair down quite literally, bucked the education system, left their homes and travelled the countryside or the wide world, sharing sex freely and using drugs to hallucinate.

In the industrial West, this generation, born at the end of the second world war, had grown up in the social security which resurgent industry provided to their relatively stable nations but often faced insecurity in their home environments because of the traumas their parents had lived through during the war. Whatever the reasons for their movement, that generation, as a whole, indulged in more freedom and more attempts at individual fulfilment than any before — or probably ever.

They wrenched culture right out of its classical, religious and folk traditions and created new cultural forms that were young in spirit and available to all. Music was their chief medium but it was a new music, as electricity-powered instruments and drug-hyped passions created sounds that had never been heard before. They accompanied songs that spoke in the simplest terms of love, the pressures of relationships, work and the traumas of being in an industrial, automated, frenetic, urban milieu. Painting became even more pop than music for that rebellious generation of youth as the aerosol spray can replaced brush and wall replaced canvas.

There was an element of idealism in their rebellions. They demonstrated against war and called for "flower power", brotherhood among peoples and gender equality. They challenged hierarchy and dominance wherever they found it in their lives and experiences. Their movement tended to be the most egalitarian ever. Women and men shared the same experiences, life-styles and clothes and people of different races and backgrounds mixed freely, largely without prejudice.

In parts of Latin America and Asia, the fervour of the 1960s led bands of young people to agitate and lead peasants in armed struggles against the established political orders in their countries, some of them with Marxist ideological underpinnings.

Unfinished concerns

However, the large majority of that generation was not searching for solutions for the world at large, for systems that could provide equitable, just and sustainable lives for all. In the main, their search was for escape from responsibility, even for themselves, and was geared to gain as many experiences, however weird or sordid, as possible.

By the 1980s, it had become clear that most of that generation, particularly in mainline European societies, had not only returned to "the system" they had so contemptuously bucked, they had become leaders of a society dominated by industrial corporations which had entered a spiral of producing more and more products which had never been needed before they were invented.

By the 1990s, that generation had become the establishment in many of these countries. The superficiality of its youthful rebellions was nowhere better illustrated than in US President Bill Clinton's claim that he smoked dope but did not inhale it, and his attempt to gloss over his publicly demonstrating during the 1960s against the US involvement in the war in Vietnam. Taking over the administration of the US in 1992, he carried forward with ardour his predecessors' agenda of forcing open the economies of the rest of the world to US products and pushed through the establishment of a new World Trade Organization that could threaten the economic and trading interests of less powerful nations more forcefully than before.

New reality

The youth of the 1990s grew up amid far more political and economic uncertainty during the 1980s than there had been during the 1950s, and many of this generation have been overwhelmed into a robotic acceptance of the mass culture generated by the multinational corporations that increasingly dictate life-styles around the world. Others have been sucked, sullenly or cynically, into the growing underworlds of crime in cities across the globe. Still others have been drawn to fundamentalist religious movements or into ethnic wars — sometimes as mercenaries, out to enjoy themselves outside the pale of the law.

However, there are some among this generation of youth who are searching, probably more ardently than any young people have before them, for lasting answers to the problems of the world, not only for themselves but for all creatures on the earth and for those that follow them. Their concern for the future is striking. A large number of the young people at the ecumenical gathering of youth and students in Brazil in 1993 were deeply concerned — more than about solutions for themselves — about education, about how and what they should teach students, many of whom may be barely a decade younger than they are.

Those who examined the problems of providing "education for life" during the gathering expressed their concept of a life-giving, liberating education in the words of a song by the rock band, Pink Floyd: "We don't want no education, we don't want no thought control. Hey, teacher, leave those kids alone."

They were talking about liberation not only from formal controls and the kind of social taboos against which the 1960s generation rebelled, but also against the tyranny of the new mass culture, which is packaged as liberating, enriching and fulfilling for the individual, particularly the young individual, but which actually promotes the sales of more and more goods and destroys more and more of the earth and all that is in it. It leads to alienation and social breakdown among those who are drawn into it and to the impoverishment of those beyond its pale.

They were struggling with the challenge of enabling children to get out of the trap of wanting, aspiring, desiring, always for more, and having, therefore, to work and compete with the sort of soul-destroying ardour that leads to the alienation of individuals, the breakdown of families and the brutalization of societies.

They were seeking ways to bring their students to the knowledge of attitudes that would allow them to live in harmony and happiness with others around them, lead their nations to live in harmony with other nations and lead human beings everywhere to live in harmony with other creatures and with the earth and all that is in it.

Those at the gathering who started out to examine human rights and democracy, economic systems, the environment, women's concerns, the search for unity, all found themselves discussing the inter-related nature of these problems and realizing that imbalance and disharmony on each of these fronts impinge on and complicate the others.

The web of today's complex problems obviously needs comprehensive answers and perhaps it is in the minds, attitudes and knowledge of the next generation that a holistic solution to the world's ills can begin to be formed.

A Message from the Gathering

A letter to young people, our churches, our movements and organizations

In the life-giving power of the Holy Spirit, we greet you, sisters and brothers in Christ!

"We declare to you what was from the beginning, what we have heard, what we have seen with our eyes, what we have looked at and touched with our hands, concerning the Word of life... We are writing these things so that our joy may be complete" (1 John 1:1,4).

We are 524 young people from 81 countries representing ten Christian organizations. We gathered in Brazil for the Ecumenical Global Gathering of Youth and Students, 10-26 July 1993, to find a new vision for our fragile world.

We came together, an energetic, creative and resourceful people, eager to learn, study, share and act with others. We did not come with ready-made solutions but we came with a strong desire to share experiences and to work together.

The programme for the gathering included Bible study and worship, small group discussions, theme presentations, cultural celebrations and exchanges and immersion experiences into local communities. The programme also included discussions and study forums around six topics: economy, society, and alternative models; education for life; environment and development; rights of people and democracy; the search for unity in a fragmented world; and women.

Throughout our many interactions, we discovered we have much in common. We are all affected by poverty, unemployment, the world economy and violations of human rights. As youth, many of us felt a sense of powerlessness, a compassion for those excluded from decisionmaking and a deep passion for justice. This enabled us to express a special kind of solidarity with those who search for new ways of living and whose voices are seldom heard. We also celebrated our love for laughter, music and dance, and we shared our stories, tears and struggles.

We also discovered there is much that divides us. We disagreed on issues such as human sexuality, the interpretation of the Bible, different theological orientations and cultural and personal prejudices. In spite of our differences, however, we found a bond through our common humanity and faith in Jesus Christ.

Rather than fall into a repressive homogeneity, we are committed to continue to wrestle together for the unity expressed in the vision of the kingdom of God. In God's house, there is room enough for all of us. Perfect love casts out fear (John 14:2; 1 John 4:18).

We return to the communities, churches and organizations that sent us, but agonizing because we have seen and experienced the fragility of relationships and our whole creation. We return committed to being seeds of hope and transformation. We bring more than just memories, documents and experiences. We are young people touched by the power of the Spirit of God and the spirit of unity. We are transformed and we hope to be agents of transformation.

"Where there is no vision, the people perish" (Prov. 29:18). We challenge our churches and partner organizations to take us seriously *now* because we are already perishing. We covenant with you to take our power and response-abilities faithfully and to work with you for the growth and transformation of our lives and world.

We are the vision. We want to be the vision. Together, let us be the vision!

"I call heaven and earth to witness against you today that I have set before you life and death, blessings and curses. Choose life so that you and your descendants may live" (Deut. 30:19).

In Christ, EGGYS, 26 July 1993 Mendes, Brazil

The partner organizations in the EGGYS process
International Movement of Catholic Students (IMCS)
International Young Catholic Students (IYCS)
International Young Catholic Workers (IYCW)
Lutheran World Federation (LWF)
SYNDESMOS (The Fellowship of Orthodox Youth)
World Alliance of Young Men's Christian Associations (YMCA)
World Alliance of Reformed Churches (WARC)
World Council of Churches (WCC)
World Student Christian Federation (WSCF)
World Young Women's Christian Association (YWCA)

Reports from the Forums

The forums at the gathering were intended to identify the structures that generate inequality and exclusion, to develop personal plans for action related to those issues, to build up awareness of issues and experiences of struggles that would contribute to empowerment and to promote dialogue, tolerance and understanding. Each of the six forums at the gathering produced a written report, excerpts from which are included here.

Economy, society and alternative models

...The present world economy has strayed far from biblical values... The people of the developing world suffer in poverty and oppression at an ever-increasing rate. Power is becoming increasingly centralized in national elites in third-world countries, and in transnational corporations, which escape national regulation. Transnational corporations transfer wealth from the third-world countries to the rich countries through profits. The poor countries also transfer wealth to the rich countries as they finance their debt. They send more money to the rich countries to service their external debt than they receive from the rich countries in aid. Although the poor did not benefit from the original loans causing the debt, they must pay the interest on these loans through reduced government services such as health and education. The local elites work in alliance with the international financial institutions, in particular the International Monetary Fund and the World Bank. To obtain loans from the IMF, countries must follow prescribed structural adjustment programmes which are ill-suited to the variety of problems that third-world countries face. Policies that restrict government spending, devalue the currency and encourage privatization have led to unemployment, lack of education, poverty and malnutrition.

These pains are especially felt by women and youth. They find it increasingly difficult to obtain work and gain access to education at a variety of levels. In addition, women's work in the household is not valued as part of the economy. Children are further exploited through child labour and are forced into crime and prostitution.

In addition to forgetting the value of people, the economy can forget the value of God's creation. Nature is treated solely in terms of resource inputs in the economic cycle. This leads to resource depletion and environmental degradation.

Although third-world countries are largely politically independent, they still suffer under economic neo-colonialism, through the external control of the transnational corporations and international financial institutions. The idols of materialism, individualism and consumerism uphold the status quo and have prevented real change from occurring. Another idol, militarism, drains massive resources worldwide and causes civil wars in some countries, paralyzing these countries' economies...

Through mass media, cultural identity has been transformed into the life-styles and life-values of those countries with multinational corporations that impose their economic goal of a profit maximization policy. This imposition reflects a philosophy of life that is based on winners and losers, haves and have-nots and material value over human value.

Our being conscious of this economic order is the foundation that will construct and guide our search for developing alternative models of economic action in our communities, churches and organizations. We must think and work together to build social-economic transformation processes that meet the needs of our people and our right for democracy and justice...

In each of our different contexts, we see various problems through our experiences. There is, however, within these differences an inherent call to building community empowerment and unity at the local level and networking those communities to build regional and global solidarity movements.

Following the teachings of Jesus Christ, this community building entails a change in the direction of economics towards the development of humanity. This alternative model seeks a personal change in commitment to the welfare of the community and society at large...

We, as Christian youth and students, have developed a vision of processes which will lead to the advancement of justice and equality in our social, political and, in particular, our economic systems. This vision includes the development of cooperative community-based economic programmes designed to improve local economies. This empowerment at the community level will lead to an increase in the value of human life rather than productivity or wealth which has devastated many cultures and societies. This vision will facilitate equality between genders, races and regions of the world.

The vision of community cooperatives extends beyond the local level. For an international transformation of economics to occur, a network between these cooperatives must be established at the regional and international level. We must form an economic solidarity movement between the North and the South to achieve our goals of justice and equality. This network must transcend all boundaries which have in the past blocked the unity of peoples. It must extend to the north, south, east and west. And it is in this solidarity movement that we can gain back the values of cooperation and equality which have escaped us in our "free-market" society.

We believe that education must be an essential part of this transformation. Education plays a key role in the raising of consciousness against politically and economically oppressive systems. Education also provides a means by which societies and in particular youth and students can become responsible for taking a more active and democratic role in the development of a society of justice, equality and solidarity.

The church must be part of this struggle. We need to influence the church to increase its involvement in the community and the economy. The church is a very important place for consciousness-raising and education. The church must not become comfortable with its position in society. It must continually fight for the rights of the common citizen and practise the teachings of Jesus Christ.

Together, we have visioned; we have discussed solutions to our problems. Now is the time for us, Christian youth and students, to act. We are the present and the future; we are change. The world is waiting for our strength and our ideas. We can fight in a spirit of unity. We are the solution. We are the vision. We are the action.

Women

Women from different countries of the world suffer under similar situations of oppression and of violation of their basic rights... As we organized the information collected during the course of the women's forum, we identified different aspects of women's lives in society:

1. Social

A. Ethnic-racial: Within the social structures in all the regions in which we live, ethnic-racial recognition and respect is needed for individuals. A stereotype is imposed on the women in our countries that says they should be perfect and beautiful, have light skin, be tall, have light eyes and "well-turned out" figures. This often means that those who do not look like this are unable to get good jobs, even when they are professionally qualified.

In our church organizations and ecumenical groups, there is a lack of concrete, specific policies and programmes that lead us to racial equality...

B. Religion: A group of women gather together to sew, to quilt, to bake, to clean and to cater meals. They will be genuinely appreciated for their contributions, but they do not serve communion, take the offering or serve as treasurer, president of the church council or minister. They will be explicitly or implicitly excluded from leadership in the church. Churches participate in politics of oppression by not providing leadership role models for young women in churches, by excluding biblical stories of women or biblical stories about the liberation of women and by appreciating women only for their contribution as care-givers and fund-raisers... The church is often the main element in reinforcing the patriarchal family structure that convinces women they are inferior to men in the home, in their financial life, etc.

C. Education: For us as women, education has become an element for continuing the roles that society has established for us in the family and through the media. Women have little access to technical professional training that could help raise our level of life in the political, economic and social arenas. We often cannot choose the careers that we would like most...

D. Family and raising children: The model of the patriarchal family found in our societies has given women a limited social role subject to men's desires... The social roles of the patriarchal family assign women the task of educating and raising the children and caring for the home (cleaning, cooking, shopping, etc.). Men are charged with economically maintaining the home. Today, this picture is being increasingly questioned with the presence of women in many professions. Women inevitably are caught in the contradiction between the desire to work and the "obligation" to care for the home...

E. Health: There are numerous social ills that affect a woman's health. These may have a negative impact on her mental and physical well-being. In most cases they are direct results of "myths" and ignorance. Many women are not adequately educated on health issues. Of specific concern to us in the women's forum were the issues of women with AIDS, adequate pre-natal care for pregnant women, breast cancer, access to safe and legal abortion, access to and information about different methods of contraception, menopause, substance abuse and breast-feeding.

F. Homophobia: Homophobia is the fear and hatred of homosexual men and women. It is widespread throughout society and our churches. Homophobia hurts all people because it denies the opportunity for dialogue. Many lesbian women and gay men are deeply affected by homophobia. It denies them a voice in church and society. It segregates and isolates them. Homophobia denies homosexuals the opportunity to be honest about their lives, their thoughts and their feelings. It can also lead to harassment and violence... We recognize that the issue of sexuality and homosexuality is one that many churches struggle with, and yet we are called to end oppression. It is not always easy for Christians to recognize that homophobia is oppression.

G. Violence: Violence against women is a reality that crosses all lines of race, class, ethnicity, sexual orientation and culture. All women are vulnerable to becoming victims of violence. This violence, of course, manifests itself in different ways in different contexts... *Sexual harassment* is a behaviour of a sexual nature that is unwanted — looks, touching, jokes, showing sexual materials, standing too close, making sexual innuendos or threats for favours... *Incest* is any sexual relationship between two members of a family who are not married to one another. Most often it is perpetrated by an older male relative (father, uncle, brother). Incest is a manipulative and violent expression of sexuality and power that often permanently scars its victims. *Rape* is... one of the most prevalent forms of violence against women and can be perpetrated by a stranger, a friend or an acquaintance. In war situations women and young girls are particularly vulnerable to rape since soldiers often view rape as one of the "privileges" of war. *Prostitution* is exchanging sexual acts for material or economic gain... The increasing incidence of child prostitution should call our churches to action in trying to help eradicate this problem. *Pornography*... can be physical like rape or it can be the objectification of the body... for sexual gratification. The advertising industry consistently uses sexuality and the objectification of women to sell products. *Clergy sexual abuse* occurs when members of the clergy are sexually involved with members of their congregation or other people who with whom they are relating as a pastor... The power dynamics involved often make it impossible for true mutuality to occur in such relationships. These relationships are abusive...

H. Sexuality:... Sexuality is much broader than sexual relations. It includes how we treat our bodies, how we respect ourselves in relationship with others, and it includes our God-given feelings for each other as friends, colleagues, family and partners/spouses...

In many countries young girls are bombarded with media images of slim, provocative women and often assume this is the expected way to express their sexuality. When women and young girls accept the media portrayal of women as ideal, they are often feel unhappy about their own bodies or they act out sexually in ways that leave them feeling lonely and isolated. Our society and our churches contribute to the confusion by silencing young women who want to talk about their sexuality and how the church's teachings relate to media and cultural influences...

2. Political

A. Leadership and training for change: Due to the way that labour has traditionally been divided into gender-specific roles women have often not had the opportunity to serve in leadership roles in the church, in their communities and in their organizations. We have personally experienced the empowering effect that leadership training has had on our own lives and we have witnessed its effect in the lives of women with whom we work. Women often bring new ideas and experiences into their leadership positions based on their own personal experience and their situation as a woman in the world. Women also often bring a new vision of power-sharing into their leadership roles and into their communities and organizations... We feel very strongly that leadership development of young women and girls should be a priority of our organizations and our churches...

B. Laws that discriminate against women: Politics of oppression are everywhere, and can often be found institutionalized by our governments through laws that discriminate against women or harm women... Women are often discriminated against in property laws in that they cannot buy, own or inherit property. In many countries it is legal for a husband to rape his wife and for courts to use a woman's past sexual history as evidence against her in cases where she has been a victim of a sexual assault...

C. Women's rights as human rights: Because women are often viewed as second-class citizens, laws that discriminate against women or are harmful to women are ignored or justified. It is important to understand that struggles for women's rights are struggles for human rights and that the struggle is for justice and equality and not a struggle for special status or for superiority.

D. Lobbying and monitoring women's issues: Because there are so many laws that discriminate against women and because women often do not receive fair trials or adequate support when they are being oppressed, it is important to monitor women's issues and struggles on a worldwide basis. Lobbying and letter-writing campaigns can help show governments that people all over the world are aware of the situation in their country...

E. Church's role in politics: In the diversity of our nationalities, denominations, movements and life experiences the one thing that pulls us together is our profession of faith. In our Christian tradition we share the power of the gospel of Jesus Christ and his example to us of seeking out the poor and oppressed in society. The church has a responsibility to be pro-active in our world in trying to help establish the new community of God here in our midst. We have a responsibility to call our governments in to accountability and intervene on behalf of people wherever they are being oppressed. We must always remember that it is our faith and our God who call us to action.

3. Economic

A. Employment: Many women in all cultures are still bound by traditional roles that do not allow women (or make it harder for women) to pursue careers in fields that have been dominated by men... Even when women are well-qualified they often have more difficulty in finding a job and in advancing in their career... Particularly in an age when so many families are single-parent households headed by women, women need to have access to jobs that pay enough to provide for themselves and their families. Women have the additional problem of sexual harassment in the work-place, often with no support or avenues for justice. Women also often do not have access to education so that they might be able to pursue the careers that they dream of... Sexual harassment and low wages hit poor women harder because they are often more dependent on their jobs and are thus more vulnerable to exploitation without having access to any recourse for justice...

B. Women's unpaid work: People often do not appreciate or fully comprehend the work-load that women face. People take for granted the tasks that go unnoticed every day but that would shut down society if women refused or could not perform them. These tasks include cooking, cleaning, washing clothes, gardening, raising children, etc... These responsibilities need to be recognized by society as essential and our economic and governmental policies must change to reflect this attitude...

C. Pay equity: The fact that men and women rarely receive equal pay for equal work is simply a matter of discrimination, and our churches should be active in helping to create justice for women in this area...

D. Child care: The responsibility of caring for and raising children needs to be recognized to be that of both the mother and the father as well as the community. As members of a community and as Christians, we have a responsibility to ensure that the children in our midst grow up in safe and loving environments... Because so many parents are working these days, we should see child care as an important and effective way to tackle this problem...

E. Women and the world economy: The structural economic adjustment policies aimed at satisfying the demands of a business group have an unequal impact on the poorest people of the world, a negative impact on all youth, children and elderly, but especially on women... As women have had to integrate themselves in great numbers to the informal economy that offers them no social guarantees, they also enter into competition at home, ending in a high level of exploitation at home, at work and at all levels of society.

* * *

In our experience as a women's forum... many expressed their frustration that they feel isolated from other women who share their struggles and their point of view. We experienced the empowerment of sharing our stories and our experiences and finding out that other women shared our opinions, passions and desire to work towards transforming our society into a more just society of equality and respect for women and men...

We desire to work in partnership with men, and we believe that we were not dealing with "women's issues", as each and every one of these issues are relevant to both men and women. While we do believe very strongly that patriarchy is the root of many of these problems, in stating this we are not attempting to blame individual men or to promote male-bashing. We believe that patriarchy is a system of oppression that oppresses both women and men although it manifests itself differently in its oppression of men from in its oppression of women. Patriarchy often keeps men separated from their feelings and alienated from their families, particularly their children. It often places incredible pressure on men to succeed in their careers, and this is often measured in terms of monetary compensation. Patriarchy often teaches misogyny (the hatred of women) and leads to the creation of an environment in which men do not respect women or view them as partners in creation.

"Where there is no vision, the people will perish." We believe we do have a vision and we cannot wait until that vision becomes reality. It is our responsibility to usher in the new community of God. It is our responsibility to voice our vision, to share that vision and work together to make it a reality. The vision that we have is the vision of a new society in which women and men truly live as co-creators with each other. A world in which women and men respect each other and work together on solving their problems. Our vision is of a world where women and young girls are safe, where our bodies are not objictified and where our sexual choices can be made in a loving, Christian context and respected by others. Our vision is of a world where women have equal access to education and to the careers of their choice and a world where men share the division of labour at home and share equally in both the joys and the responsibilities of raising children...

Education for life

Education is a positive, growing experience for life and humanization, through socialization. It is the means to transmit values and knowledge in order to obtain information and power... It is necessary for the conservation of cultural values...

The situation of education in our societies

Education is seen as a privilege and not as a right. There are not enough schools, especially public schools. In some third-world countries, the public schools only offer primary education, as there are no secondary schools available for the continuation of studies. Young people are educated as future manual labourers instead of as thinking individuals. Education is being directed towards a certain group of persons, not for the whole society equally. Many children drop out of school because they must work to help their families financially.

Free formal education is inadequate for all members of society. This has resulted in student movements that try to reverse this situation because it does not lead to a holistic education of persons that can awaken their interest in the social context. However, there are few people involved in this kind of movement.

The conditions of educational facilities are inadequate. Classrooms are not large enough and there are not enough of them, forcing the students sometimes to have classes outside under the trees.

On the other hand, there are countries that have free education at the secondary and university levels. In these countries, much is demanded of the students from an early age, producing much emptiness and stress, and resulting in their alienation. There is a great amount of competition for the openings at the higher levels of education.

One problem found in all the countries is the low pay for teachers, causing some to lose interest in improving the quality of the instruction they offer. Sometimes they have to strike to demand their rights, leaving the students without classes. Also in many countries there is a high rate of illiteracy.

What kind of education do we want?

...Our goal is a holistic education for the individual, which trains one with a critical conscience. Students should be seen as subjects for change who can secure their own education, which aims towards the creation of a democratic and more just society.

We want an education that articulates the means necessary for individuals to be aware of the realities of different countries, the distinct social movements, and then, based on this information, to confront their own ideas and have a more critical and constructive view of society. It is essential to be responsible actors in our lives, leaders, militants, in order to be agents for change.

We consider education as the promotion of a professional vocation for a life valued for and by society; as our own socialization and promotion of a life in community, accessible for all and with the necessary resources; as the means to ensure development of an opposition to war, violence, drug addiction, etc.; as the acquisition of knowledge and power, not only as a means to get a job, but for life and life in fullness.

Our commitment to action

We should reformulate our actions as youth groups, updating our structures to generate commitment and to meet the needs of youth:

— inform and educate about just values, taking social changes into account;
— join forces in order to have joint work among the organizations;
— the struggle to change the educational system is a very broad struggle, and should take place in a social context, engaging the efforts of diverse social and youth groups, focusing on specific social problems...

Environment and development

...As youth, many of us feel a sense of powerlessness and a sense of compassion for those excluded from decision-making. This has hopefully enabled us to express a special kind of solidarity with those whose voices are seldom heard and those who search for new ways of living.

We meet at EGGYS realizing that human beings are created of the same matter by God, and have special responsibilities for the stewardship of creation. What God has given us should be used to serve and to enrich our lives, but should not be used to fulfil our greed and to dominate others...

At the outset, participants discussed their own experiences and local contexts... Small groups offered creative presentations to the forum as a whole, underlining the main issues of concern and the specific problems they wished to tackle:

— nuclear testing, nuclear wastes and contamination, especially in the Pacific region:
— ocean and fresh-water pollution, particularly due to contamination by toxic chemicals;

— deforestation leading to soil erosion, climate change, desertification and diminished natural beauty;
— population concerns, particularly the need to empower women with education and resources for sustainable development;
— over-consumption in richer areas of the world which consume proportionally much more than their fair share of the world's resources;
— the inefficiency of the United Nations Conference on Environment and Development (UNCED) to deal effectively with the urgent problems facing the earth;
— the apparent lack of motivation on the part of established networks, international organizations and even churches to deal with these same problems;
— the contradictions between beliefs and actions apparent in our own lives and at the EGGYS meeting itself...

Participants in the forum on environment and development wished to emphasize action and commitments rather than documentation in a final report... Young people at EGGYS realized that what was needed was not only rectification of certain identifiable problems, but also a conversion of individuals to new attitudes towards nature, other human beings and to new willingness to act.

Finally, the young people at EGGYS decided that the most effective means of presenting their work to the gathering as a whole was through a set of commitments to principles and to action which we promise to undertake both personally and collectively:

1. We commit ourselves to the search for abundant life, for all of God's creation, and we struggle against the structures that cause death in general and in concrete ways.
2. We commit ourselves, as concerned young people, to devote our energy, creativity and new perspectives to

the difficulties we face, to take responsibility for the situations we can change and to inspire others with hope in the possibility of change.

3. We commit ourselves, as Christians, to God's plan for the beauty and integrity of the natural world and the right for every person to live as full a life as possible.

4. In order to implement the commitments expressed above, we will:

   a) change our own personal habits and daily behaviours, remembering that such modifications provide not only examples for others but also express our solidarity with the commitments we have made at EGGYS and the world that they effect;

   b) educate ourselves and others; only by understanding the inter-relations between, for example, poverty, environmental degradation, the status of women and the hegemony of capitalism are we empowered to act and to convince others to be protagonists in effecting change;

   c) protest through acts of personal and collective defiance that express our dissatisfaction with the world we live in now and our desire to bring about change;

   d) join with others in local, regional and international networks, sharing information with partners around the world, especially those young people we have encountered at EGGYS...

Rights of people and democracy

Theology of human rights and democracy

The Bible represents the historic journey of God's people illuminated by their faith. They have had a number of very different ways of organizing their societies, but none of these has been presented as a model... God has not given humanity a specific plan for social organization... Even when Jesus preached about the kingdom, he did not present a definite model for society.

What we can find in the Bible is a series of values that shed light on how to build a society: solidarity, community values and justice. However, it is not possible to extract the democratic system as such from the Bible.

God's plan always questions human social systems. That is why it always resists legitimizing them... The problem of our societies is the pluralism resulting from so many cultures and religions. Therefore, we need to base the building of society on universal values that can be accepted by all. The Bible can be very helpful in this...

God always values those who are scorned by society. That is why the poor and marginalized are privileged people in the construction of the kingdom. Their weakness transforms them into a force for action and denunciation. This privilege does not mean that others are excluded, but rather clarifies support for this sector of society.

In our societies, there are many groups who declare that they are the true bearers of the kingdom's values. They truly are if they are effectively working for solidarity and justice. Otherwise, they are only bringing alienation and are the bearers of a plan for death. The legitimization of social systems by religions is an example of this.

As youth, we can be true agents for awareness and for change if we enter into solidarity with the poorest. If we try to follow in the footsteps of the powerful in this world, we will lose sight of the values of the kingdom and estrange ourselves from its privileges.

People's self-determination

Self-determination is where people have power over their destiny. They act individually and collectively to assert their culture, race, identity, religion, values, family life. With self-determination, a people can realize their potential, socially, politically and economically, in sustainable, life-giving societies, ensuring human dignity and ultimately life abundantly.

Racism, cultural discrimination, and the absence of peoples' rights counter any real self-determination. Full self-determination ensures the full enjoyment of people's rights.

Peoples movements are essential as the nucleus around which "civil society" emerges. People's organizations allow the voice of the "powerless" to be heard. This is the basis for united action to challenge injustice.

There is a silent racial and cultural discrimination in society. To confront this, we need changes in the way the state is organized in order to recognize diversity and cultural plurality.

Discrimination has meant the loss of traditional cultural values and thus the loss of self-determination. For indigenous peoples, self-determination is also a question of their land.

We also need to respect cultures and traditions. We should denounce the intervention and alienation of foreign cultures because they lead to the extinction of races and indigenous cultures...

We urge our groups, churches and associations to maintain contact with indigenous and ethnic groups striving to realize self-determination. Channels of support and solidarity must be formed, ready for action.

Those of us not from indigenous peoples must listen intently to the needs and hopes of the first nations, as the building of trusting relationships is essential. We seek action to transform situations... Only the respect for all peoples as human beings will enable a transformation of our countries and societies to the ethic of justice.

The democratization process

Democracy comprehends all aspects of life. Democracy is not confined to the realm of politics; it has to do with the societal as well. Democracy is present in interpersonal and social relationships. In a democracy, the people participate in the fundamental decision-making processes. Therefore, democracy cannot be narrowed to the right to vote alone. Participation in the decision-making processes is possible when basic life conditions have been guaranteed: health, education, housing, employment. In order to achieve participation, people should be educated about democracy. In short, democracy means the government of the people, by the people and for the people.

In a democracy, every person should have the right to his or her realization as a human being, i.e. every person has the same rights and opportunities; rulers must be accountable to people who elected them; the autonomy and culture of minorities are respected; the weakest are protected; and community values are reinforced vis-a-vis individualistic ones...

To be able to advance, it is important to have an ideal. It is the hope for a better world to come which keeps us alive. Democracy is a way of life. That is why democracy has to be taught, basic education is needed, the people have to be informed. For example a curriculum for democracy has to be included in the schools, which requires literacy. The two are directly linked.

It also requires a good knowledge of our respective systems. One of the ways to achieve this could be the creation of a network on two levels:

1) to create in our respective countries spaces for communication where people can exchange, be informed...;
2) to develop, on an international level, a solidarity which will allow taking common stands on common problems...

Violations of human rights and civil society
The catalogue of violated human rights is extensive:
— basic human rights to education, health and food are denied by governments as they reduce expenditure amidst structural adjustment;
— rights to democratic participation, freedom of expression and information are violated when opposition voices are not tolerated, and government-controlled radios, televisions and newspapers are imposed on the population. In its worst forms, people are tortured, killed, and detained without trial. Government control of judicial processes denies the right to fair trials;
— education for human rights is not done in most countries. People are left to decide what are their rights. Too often, even if they know their rights, they find it difficult to fight for them in the absence of solidarity around them...;
— some militant movements which initially claim to promote human rights end by practising violence, so violating rights of others... We must be clear that movements and organizations we become involved with are representative, truly popular and neither exclusive or discriminatory;
— gays and lesbians are denied their rights to live full lives in society. Women's rights are denied in various settings;
— unemployment denies young people the right to work.
People's movements are essential as the nucleus around which "civil society" emerges. It is the participation of people in them which gives legitimacy to such movements and make them work... People's movements are outlets for creative and alternative strategies to change economic crisis and political chaos. They are able to do this when they are based on the realities people live. People's organizations have an inherent possibility to create a new kind of democracy as they contribute to and

foster power-sharing and grassroots participation, with a greater equality of rights. Churches can be of significant impetus if their involvement with the people facilitates the living of faith within the context of struggle. This nurturing has both a spiritual and a practical dimension.

People's organizations allow the voice of the "powerless" to be heard. This is the basis for united action to challenge injustice.

Rights of women
...The feminist critique of societal systems which oppress women (and men), or patriarchy, is clear. Any change in the values which form the basis of the system will cause trauma in both individual and communal life. Such change will inevitably occur, however, as people are willing to hear the voices of the oppressed and remain vulnerable to the transformative power of human testimony...

Violence against women is found in all patriarchal societies. This is physical, emotional, psychological, economic and spiritual. With alarming regularity, acceptance of the violence against women is affirmed in our educative processes and media, implicitly and explicitly. Such "socially acceptable" attitudes are often played out in relationships between women and the instruments of government such as the police and military. In time, it becomes embedded in the socialization of the community. Criminalization of such violence is often the only way to overcome common law precedents which reflect an unacceptable tolerance of this violence. The voice of women in this and other parliamentary processes is sadly lacking. Christian churches have mostly failed to act in opposition to these trends, offering implicit religious approval of the denial of human rights...

Legal rights of women are upheld in many places. Practice, however, is often different from legal intent.

The length of the legal process often frustrates justice, with women withdrawing their claims due to the stress of waiting. Neglect of personal support for women involved in litigation is prevalent in the church. The Christian community, often respected by the judiciary, has a valuable opportunity to uphold the rights of its people by being willing to stand by them in litigation. Left in a position of vulnerability, women who protest against an unjust system are too often harassed...

Power structures which affect most women are geared to the advantage of those who are not in the situations which women share. Many women lose faith in the systems of power under which they live as a result of this bias. Calls for change are often met with an irrational fear that women will simply replace men at the top of the power tree... In many cases women find claiming social power impossible due to a long history of powerlessness, convincing them that subordination is an integral part of womanhood...

Relationships and the family offer women support. Too often they also offer women abuse of their rights and person. Their right to self-definition in this area is denied when the women are young, in prison, lesbian or undergoing regular medical treatment. Women often bear the greatest burden of the rising number of single parent families. In many cultures, single parenthood results in social unacceptability, especially in rural areas. New-born babies are also subjected to the spectre of female infanticide — a phenomenon in countries where caste and class systems are vicious. Such discrimination is often condoned by the silence of Christian organizations and churches.

People's movements are outlets for creative and alternative strategies to change economic crisis and political chaos. We are members of churches, youth organizations

88

and movements. But we are also part of wider movements for transformation. We weave these together in our lives...

The search for unity in a fragmented world

...Participants in our forum exchanged testimonies of struggle, hopes and experiences of the diversity of cultural, political, ethnic, economic and religious backgrounds. In each of these testimonies there existed a common experience of fragmentation. Additionally, this exchange demonstrated the great variety of realities of fragmentation...

The forum addressed the following subjects with a "global eye": women struggles, religious fundamentalism, racism, ethnocentrism and social classes. The following are some of the major contributions to the debate:

Women

Analyzing our societies with a gender approach, we realize that our predominant experience is one of patriarchal systems, where women live in a situation of inferiority and men in the position of superiority. In this situation, women suffer political, economic and social marginalization in different areas...

There exists an unspoken division within each society — one in which men are seen as masters of the external (economics, politics) world and women are responsible for the internal world (household, children's education). This makes a link between women, the third world and nature. All three become subjected to avaricious and undying exploitation. The system therefore perpetuates an inequality which manifests itself in the woman as sex object, unpaid worker and second-class citizen.

We must acknowledge women's struggles as a liberation movement in order to change the marginalized position of women in society and to balance masculinity and femininity in our societies.

Religious fundamentalism

Fundamentalism... is expressed as a rejection of modernity in the name of a security that we supposedly enjoyed in the past. Fundamentalism focuses attention on a simplistic formula, stressing only three or four basic tenets and ignoring important issues which may arise. Fundamentalism is a psycho-social attitude which can give expression to diverse ideologies: thus we have Islamic fundamentalisms, Christian fundamentalisms, Marxist fundamentalisms, etc.

Fundamentalism promises security and punishes dissidence in an exemplary manner. Fundamentalist groups follow an irrational logic, though some fundamentalist assertions, taken separately, may well be valid. There is always a leader who fosters discontent and promises qualitative and radical change. In this controlled, legalistic environment, the leader can become an expert in manipulation and demagogy. The leader becomes a symbol even in prison or in death.

What can we do about this? We should be mindful of the political allegiances these groups make, the attempts to inculcate their teachings and policies in schools and their influence on legal and political systems, and, wherever a concentration of power exists, seek alliances with the victims of fundamentalism, deepen debate without discrimination of source material, and try to relate on a personal basis with fundamentalists to dispel fears, because when fear dies, hope is born...

Racism and ethnocentrism

Racism is a widespread and pervasive problem in our societies... throughout the world. In some instances, racism was a consequence of colonialism: the conquest of the Americas heightened the concept of the white man as superior to other races (Aboriginals, Blacks, Asians). Social Darwinism uses Darwinism to justify the ideology of ethno-racial superiority.

History teaches us that each particular people or ethnic group tends to reject the cultural practices of other people. In this context, ethnocentrism is a cultural arrogance which maintains the belief that our culture is superior to others.

This belief is sustained through a systematic process whereby our values are inculcated in us in our specific cultures through family, school and social circles. While striving for tolerance and pluralism, we must have a positive view of cultural diversity.

Class division

Economic power should not be seen either as a metaphysical entity or an omnipotent reality. We must learn to discern and understand the strengths and weaknesses of economic power. The economic factor is an important dimension of social classes as economic power may foster social fragmentation. The concentration of economic power and wealth has created situations where unemployment, exploitation and marginalization run high, and where the level of frustration and anger among youth is acute.

The class struggle arises from these inequalities, although poverty as a social reality does not only derive from capitalism. The class struggle is strongest when it coincides with ethnic and racial struggles. Now, due to a combination of factors (educational level or organization) the most oppressed are not necessarily the ones who struggle most.

Under the guise of information distribution, the mass media continue projecting the idea of a "superior culture", alienating people and perpetuating the dominant ideology through its sensationalism and consumerism...

* * *

In the discussion, each individual gave a positive value to diversity as a powerful expression of the richness of humankind. We celebrated our diversity and the spirit of growth which accompanies it. Diversity brings out a challenge to us all to broaden our experience, thereby allowing us to realize our full capacity as individuals, communities and nations.

Fragmentation on the other hand is negative. It suppresses the human's potential to consolidate personal, intercultural relationships on one hand, and international dialogue and understanding on the other. Fragmentation.. forces the individual and the collective into a spirit of mistrust and disrespect for "the other". Furthermore, fragmentation attempts to establish an homogeneous yet exclusivist culture. Fragmentation is the consequence of greed and selfishness. In conclusion, we come to know and understand fragmentation as alienation — indeed the result of original sin — from God and each other...

True unity is an active process which begins with respect. In the ecumenical struggle, we are made equal through this respect. Like the Godhead, unity points the way to an acceptance of differences in a spirit of trust, honesty and love. It allows for independence and self-determination and is enriched and not threatened by diversity. Built on the analysis of openness to differences, unity does not try to homogenize. Unfortunately, it is often the case that unity becomes manipulated in an attempt to draw the masses into a climate of passivity and dependence. This false unity hates diversity yet uses it to promote the

values of the powerful. As a final point, it must be
stressed that unity is not an event but a daily journey;
sometimes we find it, and sometimes it finds us. Unity is
always under construction.

For Christians, unity is commensurate with our faith
journey. In this context, we deeply regret that churches
have not always shown a paradigm of unity amidst so
much fragmentation and that this lack of unity has become
a major obstacle in evangelization, prophetic witness and
service to the world...

Three Personal Testimonies

For me, EGGYS did not only mean a place for young people from different cultures, languages and youth and student Christian organizations to share their life experiences. Nor was it the place for finding solutions to the problems that affect all of us on a global scale. It was mostly an opportunity for learning to live amidst so much diversity, for learning to tolerate and respect each other despite our differences.

For me, the highest point of the event was this opportunity to express and to feel the suffering, the joys and the dreams of other young people — and it was particularly true during the exposure programme. Through these exchanges we learned how much we are enriched by our diversity and that God created human beings to live out this diversity in community.

There were times of deep analysis during the Gathering in which we attempted to understand how and by what means our present reality can be changed... Even if we did not find or propose "solutions", our respective organizations are now much more aware of the importance of continued searching for concrete answers to those issues.

Part of this awareness is the comprehension that changes can only be brought about through the work of the entire community. Therefore, the seed of EGGYS should find its place at the grassroots so that the process towards change can be effective and truly democratic...

I do not know what will happen to me, or where each of us will be ten years from now — when we won't be youth any longer — but I only hope that once in a while we shall tackle these challenges and remind ourselves that we together became a formidable force for transformation.

What a different world it would be if we were representing our respective countries at the United Nations! The energy, the enjoyment and the way of doing politics would be rather different — for I am sure that many of us, as myself, have personally been changed by this meeting concerning our understanding of other people's cultures and values...

Paulina Quezada, Chile

...If I were to draw a chart depicting the feelings and emotions that I have experienced during my involvement in the EGGYS process..., I can say that these have been numerous. There have been some fulfilling moments when together with others from the EGGYS partner organizations we shared a clear, common vision for a better Kenya — a Kenya that was struggling with the problems of multipartyism, corruption and an educational system that is not relevant for the citizens.

We shared a clear common vision for a better Africa too — an Africa that was struggling with the issues of democracy, corruption, famines, wars and leaders who lack accountability and transparency. We shared a clear common vision for better organizations — organizations that were wrestling with the issue of youth demanding for their right to decision-making.

We shared a clear common vision for a better world — a world that was at the time divided in various ways.

There were triumphant moments when we were able to come together in solidarity actions in spite of our different cultural, denominational and organizational backgrounds. I remember the many petitions signed, the joint theological reflections, the songs, the dances, the laughter. These will remain in my memory for a long time.

The EGGYS road however has not been an easy one. There were times, and God knows they were many, when I felt frustrated, moved to anger and to tears. These were the times when we permitted our personal interests to blind our vision for a better society. Many were the times when we allowed our policies and structures, formulated and built by ourselves, to become hindrances in our endeavour to make this vision a reality.

These were the moments when I was faced with a choice to make. They were choice situations where it would have seemed better, easier or wise to pick the lightest load... or simply to give up on the whole EGGYS process.

However, I am grateful that even when I felt hopeless, alone and discouraged there were people who constantly encouraged me to move on and not to give up on the struggle...

I believe that the aim of planting the ecumenical tree was so that it may take root, grow and bear fruit. I plead with you, please let us not uproot this tree.

For me the seed has been planted. It is my challenge to take root, to grow, and to bear fruit. Will you support me?

Lillian Owiti, Kenya

Taking on a concrete commitment to continue the work begun constitutes a major task that we fear we may not be able to accomplish. We labour under the mistaken idea that we will be at the centre of major changes, not only personally, but together with those around us as well. The simple things are, however, the most difficult and are what we seek the least.

A Portuguese poet of the last century expressed in the following way what I wish to assume as my personal commitment: "If only I never had to die, but could eternally seek perfection in all things!" In other words, seeking small ways in which to change our daily attitude.

Our organizations, our movements and our churches will be the channels of information and education in this constant search, affording us spaces in which we can share and experience ecumenism and where we will not be indifferent to our fellow human beings. This dialogue often produces disagreement, creating fears that lead us to close ourselves to that very dialogue. It is therefore important to encourage tolerance and respect for others, which includes not only people, but the entire creation. It is only in that way that we will realize the importance of the little things...

Miguel Marujo, Portugal

Appendix 4

A Message to the Gathering

From Konrad Raiser, General Secretary
of the World Council of Churches

...Whatever your background, you have come together for the first world meeting of Christian youth and students in several decades, in order to manifest your longing for more ecumenical solidarity across national and ethnic, cultural and confessional lines. There is only one ecumenical movement which includes all those who want to respond in faith, life and witness to the prayer of our common Lord "that they all may be one so that the world may believe" and who "seek to fulfil together their common calling to the glory of the one God, Father, Son and Holy Spirit".

Since its beginnings, the ecumenical movement has tried to be sensitive to the voices of young people and students. It has been nourished by the commitment of young people who have challenged the churches to genuine renewal and who have been in the forefront of the struggles for justice, democratic participation and the defence of human rights.

But as you know well enough, young people, who constitute more than half of the world's population, are most exposed to hunger and disease, violence and oppression. They are forced to fight the wars of the powerful and are deprived of education and meaningful work. Many ask: Is there a future for us?

The ecumenical movement certainly has no future without the young generation. In this present period of change and transition in church and society worldwide, your gathering has the unique chance to provide orientation and inspiration to young people in the churches. You can strengthen the network of ecumenical cooperation between Christian youth movements and organizations, which has emerged in the process of preparation for EGGYS. You could thus create an important instrument for mutual support and making the voice of young people clearly heard in the ecumenical movement. In this endeavour, I wish you courage and determination, and assure you on behalf of the World Council of Churches of our prayerful support.